DEBT-FREE ASAP!

Debt-Free ASAP!

Copyright © 2020 John Nicholas. All Rights Reserved.

No part of this publication may be reproduced, stored in a retrieval system or transmitted, in any form or by any means—electronic, mechanical, photocopying, recording, or otherwise—without prior written permission from the publisher, except for the inclusion of brief quotations in a review.

DISCLAIMER:

This book is dedicated to helping readers address and eliminate their debt in the fastest, most ethical and beneficial way possible. However, no results can be promised or guaranteed. This book is also committed to helping readers better understand personal finances in general, and their own personal finances in particular, but cannot promise or guarantee any such understanding or resulting financial success or improvement. Results will vary depending on variables that are beyond the reach and responsibility of the author and/or publisher. Meanwhile, any persons, conversations or case histories described in this book are based on actual people whose names have been changed and their circumstances modified, combined to form composite characters or edited for brevity or narrative quality.

Book Interior and E-book Design by Amit Dey
Cover design by Cruzial Designs

For information about this title or for bulk orders, contact the publisher:

Nicholas Group Publishing
McKinney, Texas
Email: support@debt-freeasap.com

ISBN: 978-1-7361587-0-8 (print)
ISBN: 978-1-7361587-1-5 (eBook)

Publisher's Cataloging-In-Publication Data
(Prepared by The Donohue Group, Inc.)
Names: Nicholas, John, 1959- author.
Title: Debt-Free ASAP! : [how to know your options, create a plan & start changing your life within 48 hours] / John Nicholas.
Description: McKinney, Texas: Nicholas Group Publishing, [2021] | Subtitle from cover.
Identifiers: ISBN 9781736158708 (print) | ISBN 9781736158715 (ebook)
Subjects: LCSH: Finance, Personal. | Debt. | Consumer credit.
Classification: LCC HG179 .N53 2021 (print) | LCC HG179 (ebook) | DDC 332.024/02--dc23

DEBT-FREE
ASAP!

JOHN NICHOLAS

Nicholas Group Publishing
McKinney, Texas

Table of Contents

Dedication: Grandpa's Big Debt vii

Introduction: Why This Book? My Pandemic Detour
at the Lake ix

Part I – Your Condition 1

Chapter 1 Why Debt Sucks But Debt-Free Is Sexy 3

Chapter 2 How You Got Here 11

Chapter 3 Your Debt Load, Net Worth, P&L & FICO 17

Chapter 4 Your Debt-Free Mindset, Spirit & Vision 33

Part II – Your Options 41

Chapter 5 The Hi-Low Payoff Plan 43

Chapter 6 Debt Consolidation 49

Chapter 7 Hardship Payment Plans 57

Chapter 8 Family Assistance 63

Chapter 9 Debt-Settlement 71

Chapter 10 Bankruptcy Chapters 7 & 13 77

Chapter 11 Status Quo (Do Nothing) 85

Part III – Your Plan 89

Chapter 12 Pick an Option, Create a Plan 91

Chapter 13	Scams, Cars, Collection Calls & More	99
Chapter 14	The Support You Need to Succeed	107
Chapter 15	Keep Your Eyes on the Prize!	111

DEDICATION

Grandpa's Big Debt

My grandfather John Prassas came to America as a Greek immigrant in the early 1900's and settled with his brothers in Chicago where they hustled to sell flowers on busy street corners.

Over the years their dreams, skills and connections grew and they became prosperous real estate developers who built some of America's first shopping centers. In the process however, the Great Depression threw my grandfather into a million dollars' worth of debt, which was a heck of a lot back then.

Digging out of that massive hole took him many years and it cost him his marriage and disbursed his family, as my grandmother moved to Los Angeles with my father and his sister. As a result of long distances and strained relationships I would only meet my grandfather a couple times over the years.

But even without a relationship I was proud of my grandpa and his story; that he had been a poor immigrant turned pioneering builder who achieved success, overcame adversity and later recovered to live in a stately mansion on Sheridan Drive, Chicago's premier address overlooking Lake Michigan.

My grandfather's old home is now a Registered Historic Home that I have proudly showed to my wife and kids including our daughter who, in a romantic twist of fate, attended the University of Chicago's prestigious School of Law.

In the end, my grandfather's life presents both a cautionary tale and an inspirational story as it demonstrates both the destructive power of debt and the hope we have to overcome it.

INTRODUCTION

Why This Book?
My Pandemic Detour at the Lake

A text message pinged my phone as I sat by the pool in my back-yard. It said, "Got any gift ideas for Father's Day?" It was from my always thoughtful daughter the non-profit attorney in New York City, checking in and looking ahead to the coming holiday weekend.

"Thank you for asking!" I texted back after pausing a minute, "I'll send you a photo later." I knew that would pique her curiosity.

Would I send her a picture of a battery-powered leaf blower or a turbo-charged V-8 convertible?

Both of these objects had actually crossed my mind with a smile when my wife asked me the same question a couple days earlier. But I had a very different idea in mind for my annual Father's Day gift. And I was hoping my daughter, sons and/or wife would pitch in to help make it happen.

A COVID-19 WRITER'S RETREAT

The photo I sent my daughter showed a little lakeside cabin for rent near Gun Barrel City, Texas, an hour Southeast of Dallas. This is where I wanted to spend a few days of solitude on the back porch or under a shade tree staring out over the open water, far away from "sheltering-in-place" with my lovely wife, lovable dogs and ever-loving distractions. It was there that I wanted to do some soul searching, praying, planning and most of all...some writing.

The need for soul-searching stemmed from the world's grave condition as we battled to survive the coronavirus outbreak and its resulting medical and economic devastation while massive rallies and unrest swept the globe to protest the heart-breaking deaths of George Floyd and other tragic victims of excessive police force.

These historic events compelled me to look at my life and dig for ways to serve the world in whatever way I could, and to hopefully leave a legacy of service for my children, grandchildren, friends and neighbors.

My need for prayer was linked to all of the above plus my need for direction; what to plan and what to write as I sensed a strong leading toward a new business, a new book and a new season of life. But which business and which book?

There were several business concepts begging for my attention and even more book projects barking for my affection.

When I drove to the lake a week after receiving my requested Father's Day gift I actually took a list of *nine* partially developed book projects with me including three inspirational titles, three on personal development plus two novels and a memoir about a life-changing experience during my youth called *Beach Bully*.

I can tell you that each project is beautiful or powerful in its own way but like children you love in their own special way; it can be difficult to pick a favorite!

Hence, I was seeking guidance most of all about which book to hunker down and finally write.

THE DETOUR BOOK TOUR

That guidance arrived when I arrived at the cabin and saw the beautiful blue lake and afternoon sun blazing behind it and sensed a U-turn in the making.

Suddenly my determination to write was fading fast. And just as quickly, I felt prompted to *read* a book – not write one – during my stay.

"Well, so much for my writer's retreat!" I complained to myself in a huff as I considered the idea of making *zero progress* on any of my book projects as I entered the cabin, then sat on the back porch and tried to let the scenery calm me down.

What was I supposed to read? The rental cabin didn't have much to offer and the only book I brought along was an old paperback I had found buried in a bathroom drawer the day before when my wife and I cleaned out our vanity cabinets to prepare for a remodeling project. It had been buried under business cards, old receipts and a bunch of other junk for years.

I had tossed the book onto my travel bag in the closet just to get it out of the way but later tucked it into the bag without even thinking about it, where it traveled to the lake with me like a stowaway hiding in the bowels of a ship. Apparently the book's title, *Secrets of the Millionaire Mind* had caught my subconscious eye.

As soon as I started reading the 2005 bestseller by T. Harv Eker, a successful businessman-turned-seminar trainer, it hooked me like a large-mouth bass off one of the docks behind my cabin.

The book speaks to our deeply held "financial blueprints" that are often based on poor examples, bad experiences and negative beliefs that hinder us financially. Eker then helps us correct those beliefs by pursuing and continually reinforcing the basics of financial success. His insights are timeless; I recommend his book highly and I've already stolen some of his best stuff! Just kidding, but I will share a few of his insights as we go, giving credit where it's due.

MY WATERFRONT WAKE-UP

What the book did for me besides provoke some financial reflection of my own was re-awaken my concern for people in financial distress due to debt.

These are the people I had gotten to know from every place, background and situation imaginable, when I worked briefly in the debt-settlement industry and tried to help them. Unfortunately, I was handcuffed by limited programs featuring one-size-fits-all services or intense one-call-close tactics not to mention massive fees, limited disclosures and sometimes traumatic outcomes for clients.

These people and millions of others who struggle with debt had never left my heart, even after I left the industry. Their need for simple yet professional guidance had haunted me. That need was now fast becoming an emergency situation in the midst of the growing economic crisis.

A year or so earlier I had even outlined a book and business concept to meet this need, but that book wasn't currently on my "radar" or on the list of projects I had brought to the lake.

But now it was front and center.

Somehow the combination of Eker's book, the economic crisis and my deep-seated concern for debt-ravaged people in need of help created a 4th of July-style fireworks display in my spirit, as creative thoughts and plans sizzled, streaked, sparked and boomed for two days straight, re-igniting the vision I had left behind.

HERE WE GO

And so I started detailing the book you now hold in your hands (or now read on your screen or hear through your earphones) as well as my coaching and consulting company Debt-Free ASAP, right there at the lake.

As you will learn, both this book and my company provide a simple yet powerful 3-step process we call our "ASAP Protocol" to:

1. Assess your situation,
2. Review your options and
3. Create the best plan for your unique situation, with as much coaching support as you want or need to succeed.

This book is structured in three sections to follow this protocol. Each section is vitally important whether you're a newly minted college graduate with hefty student loans, long-retired grandparents with reduced income or any single, couple, family person or professional in-between who is struggling with debt.

The first section will help you see your situation with sober clarity, fresh perspective and through the lens of powerful tools that will help you think and act like a millionaire as you move forward. We will also seek to repair some of the damage debt may have done to your mindset, spirit and vision for your future.

You may be tempted to jump ahead of this first section to quickly review the top debt-relief solutions outlined in the second section so you can hurry up and start getting out of debt. But I exhort you to "do first things first!"

The third and final section will help you create an action plan for success very quickly, with an eye toward making sure you have the time-proven support and outlook necessary to vanquish your debt once and for all. And that is no easy task. So I hope you'll devour that section like your favorite dessert once we get there!

This simple 3-step process is what electrified my spirit at the lake that weekend as I considered how it could help you and so many others.

When my wife joined me on the third day and listened to my story, she laughed out loud then fought back tears as she recognized the amazing grace and grand irony of my detour, for reasons you will understand better as we go.

On the very next page, in fact, you will learn why this subject hits so close to home for my wife and I, and why it might do the same thing for you, and why our journey together will be so promising and hopefully so life-changing.

PART I
YOUR CONDITION

CHAPTER ONE

WHY DEBT SUCKS BUT DEBT-FREE IS SEXY

My heart was racing as I sat alone in my home office up past midnight again, rubbing my eyes, and trying not to hyperventilate as I stared at my computer screen.

On the screen was a seemingly immovable, indestructible and very long list of credit cards and other debts that were sucking the life out of me and my family. I studied them closely every night, ever mindful of the proverb that says:

> *"The rich rule over the poor and the borrower is slave to the lender."*

As an experienced entrepreneur I knew a thing or two about finances but I didn't know what to do about my situation. I was too embarrassed to talk with friends or family and had even tried working with a debt-consolidation program but couldn't keep up with the payments.

Bankruptcy looked like my only option but I couldn't afford to hire an attorney to file the forms. Even the cheapest ones ran a thousand dollars or more, so that wasn't happening.

Heck, I was digging coins out of my car's ash tray just to buy gas!

So I researched how to file a BK (the term for bankruptcy among industry insiders) all by myself. As I searched for information I berated myself for being such a colossal failure and stupid loser. How could I let debt suck me into such a hopeless black hole? How did I get to where I was in the first place?

WHEN THE TOWERS WENT DOWN

Just a year or so earlier I was making six figures and jetting around the country meeting with fancy ad agencies and Fortune 500 sponsors for the sports media and marketing company I had co-founded with a friend.

But when the World Trade Towers went down during the terrorist attacks of 9/11/2001, so did advertising and sponsorship sales for our company. Potential clients were paralyzed by uncertainty and unwilling to make new commitments right when we needed them most.

One night after meeting with ad agencies in New York just a month after the towers fell, I stood near Ground Zero and watched crews working 24/7 to clear the still-steaming piles of wreckage. Standing there under eerie construction tower floodlights in the damp and chilly fog rolling off the Hudson River, I thought about the two thousand-plus souls who were lost there and wondered if I too was doomed.

I got my answer less than a year later when the Nasdaq firm that had recently acquired our company made a decision to cut overhead costs — starting with me.

My income plummeted to zero while my debt skyrocketed almost as quickly.

Then things got worse as I became a finalist in a nationwide executive search for a CEO position to lead a successful non-profit organization in Knoxville, TN. The process dragged on for several months as they reviewed all the candidates and eventually required me to fly there twice to visit their board of directors. They didn't want to rush things of course, while I was desperate to get things rolling!

This process kept me in a state of unemployable limbo while I burned through more credit card debt to pay my bills. It ultimately left me buried in debt and still unemployed as the runner-up candidate. That's right; I was their #2 choice.

Talk about feeling like a loser.

So what did I do next? I will tell you more as we go.

But before we continue, let me tell you this. Since those hellish days I have learned a lot about debt and debt relief, from my own painful experiences, from extensive research, from counseling individuals and couples as a pastor for a number of years and from working inside the debt-settlement industry.

What I have learned unequivocally is this. Debt Sucks.

Now let us count the ways.

THE FIVE DEADLIEST EFFECTS

1. **Financial** – Debt may not suck when it's used to acquire valuable assets at low interest, which is something we'll talk about later. But high interest on most consumer debt sucks most of every payment we make down the tubes and into the coffers of very happy, healthy and wealthy banks and creditors. This leaves us stuck paying high interest debts *forever* if we make minimum payments, which is just the way creditors like it and often all we can afford.

2. **Emotional** – Debt sucks the joy out of your life every day, for reasons I can't fully comprehend or quantify, but figure you already understand, firsthand. Personal defeat and hopelessness are emotions that come to mind as ones that can easily dominate all others once you're stuck

making payment after payment with little to no progress, month after month, year after year. As you heard from me earlier, debt made me feel like a loser and a failure and that's some bad emotional space to inhabit.

3. **Mental** – Debt can invade and pervade your mind, your everyday thoughts and dreams and dramatically affect your overall mindset, sometimes to the point of obsession. In my case (which may include a bit of OCD), I would sit and stare at my list of debts, doing calculations, updating balances and reformatting lists for hours at a time and would think about debt nonstop. Debt literally sucked hours of thought, brainpower and productivity if not potential genius into thin air. And that really sucks.

4. **Relational** – Debt can suck the life out of your most precious relationships, especially marriages. Surveys say most divorces are caused at least in part by financial troubles, usually involving debt. (You can read how debt affected my grandfather and me back on my Dedication page.) Debt can also damage other family members, especially children who notice everything and often internalize financial stress and judge themselves or their family members in unhealthy ways, often for life. We will discuss how to address (and reverse) these dynamics later. Debt can also isolate you behind a wall of shame, self-hatred, anger, embarrassment, self-pity, jealousy, envy or confusion. None of these are relationship boosters.

5. **Spiritual** – Whether you believe in UFOs, Nothingness, "The Universe," Star Trek, Karma, Buddha, Islam or you share my belief in God revealed through Jesus Christ you must know that debt can suck your soul straight to Hell.

And whatever you believe or imagine Hell to be like, debt can take you there as fast as lightning and keep you there till the cows come home. Why? Because as most faith traditions agree, we are created to live and walk in abundance, what Jewish folks call Shalom and Christians call "blessed." This condition goes beyond simple 'peace' to include wealth, happiness, wholeness, love and freedom. But not debt. Debt represents scarcity, poverty, desperation and slavery. Debt is the flip side of abundance in very real and concrete financial terms. Debt doesn't mean you're a bad person, doomed or cursed. It just means you need some help, some grace and some transformation. And you need it ASAP!

SO WHY IS DEBT-FREE SEXY?

Sometimes I jokingly call myself "The World's Sexiest Man in Personal Finance." Why? Because debt-free *is* sexy and I'm the man to get you there!

Is this just a gimmick or some kind of shtick?

Well, honestly yes and no. Yes, I want to cut through the clutter and draw some attention to debt-relief, and maybe even give it some sex appeal.

But no, I seriously want to loosen you up and make you laugh a little or smile a bit if I can. Remember debt steals our joy so part of our deliverance is to laugh, preferably in the face of our tormentor, Bad Debt.

You will also notice that "debt-free" rhymes with sexy if you stretch the word out a bit, like with a little French "sex-eey" spin on it. I couldn't let that synchronicity go to waste.

Have I ever had second thoughts about imparting sex appeal onto the totally unsexy subject of debt relief? No I haven't. But my wife has.

This is ironic because my wife happens to be very sexy. It's what drew me and every other guy on our high school campus to her. She was one tough, no-nonsense knockout with an athletic build and a beautiful smile on full display as a varsity cheerleader. And yes, in perhaps my most heroic feat ever I managed to win her heart and keep it beating my way now for years.

But my sexy wife is also a second-grade teacher with high standards and an eye toward modest behavior and decorum, especially around kids. She knows how to have fun of course but her protective teacher antennae went up when she heard me talking "sexy" about this book.

MY SEXY DEFINITION AND YOUR DESTINATION

So what does a sexy but concerned second-grade teacher do about a husband playing free and easy with the English language? You guessed it.

She immediately looked up the definition for "sexy" on her iPhone as I twisted in the wind, waiting for her verdict as she read silently with her lips pursed and moving ever so slightly as she read. Cute but nerve-wracking!

"Sexually suggestive or stimulating: erotic." She read aloud at last, quickly eyeing me with a stern and disapproving frown. "From Webster's Dictionary," she added like a Supreme Court Justice.

This was terrible news.

"Hmm." I replied, holding my ground for the moment. I was not some dirty old man and this was not my intended definition of sexy and I intended to fight for it. Then she continued reading.

"The informal definition is 'generally attractive or interesting. Appealing, like a sexy stock.'" She shot me a more approving look.

"Yes, of course we're talking *informal* sexy!" I confirmed. "Everyone will know that." I said with full confidence.

Finally she relaxed and chuckled as I explained why debt relief needed a new image and why I truly am the world's sexiest man.

"In personal finance, right?" she added and we both laughed.

So do you see where we're going with this? Most experts agree that sex-appeal flows mostly from confidence and I'm here to tell you that becoming debt-free will boost your confidence a hundred-fold. Just think about how being debt-free will affect you:

Financially - You will have more cash in your pocket, wallet or purse and you'll have more sitting in your bank accounts(s), ready to invest or save for travel, gifts, emergencies or whatever. And you'll be done with high interest rates sucking you dry!

Emotionally - Imagine the stress-free emotional state of having positive balances and a growing net worth, of being a winner. Imagine smiling for no reason. Imagine the weight of the world being off your shoulders!

Mentally - Just imagine thinking about positive things once in a while...things like positive bank balances (and zero credit card balances), exotic travel destinations and charitable giving...or even building your net worth like a skyscraper! And we're going to explain how you can do it.

Relationally - No matter who you are it never hurts to have more charm, magnetism or downright sex appeal, right? And how about less worrying or arguing about finances? And don't you worry about being "too sexy" around the kids, they'll figure it out!

Spiritually - I promise it will be "well with your soul" when you experience and share the blessings of being debt-free and sexy in the totally innocent definition of the word, of course!

So let's turn the page and get you moving toward this destination as if the quality of your life depends on it.

CHAPTER TWO

HOW YOU GOT HERE

Nancy was almost hysterical. She had called in hopes of getting help with her debt but when I asked her for some basic background on her situation she started crying and sharing her life saga in a stream-of-consciousness blur that involved everything from bad parents to a bad divorce to job loss to disability to rent hikes to no-good-money-borrowing kids to...

I kept waiting for her to breathe so I could politely clarify what I needed but she was on a roll and couldn't stop talking. So finally I had to just close my eyes and jump feet-first into her rant.

"Ma'am, please!" I almost yelled to interrupt her, and then softened to almost a whisper. "I am so sorry you've had to deal with so many challenges, it sounds like you've been through a lot. But please take a deep breath and I promise to help you." This seemed to stop her in her tracks, with just a few sniffles as she recovered.

"Now if you can just try to summarize your financial situation, I can take a few notes and we can go from there. Okay?"

Thankfully this was okay with Nancy. Her finances were a mess and her life was a mess but she was okay to "hit pause" long enough to quell her emotions and calmly review her situation.

Gaining some 20/20 hindsight and perspective for Nancy would be an important next-step toward her financial recovery, following her first step of reaching out for help.

THE 7 MOST COMMON CAUSES OF DEBT

After advising more than a thousand people of every age, location and socio-economic status I can tell you that 95% of people struggling with debt fall into one of the following seven categories, and frequently fall into more than one at the same time, 'a la Nancy.

We'll review these categories as a warm-up exercise for the next chapter where we'll dig into the important numbers, nuts and bolts of your financial situation. Thankfully this warm-up will be pretty easy but still quite helpful.

After all if you're going to properly assess your situation, it will help to be clear about how you got here, right?

So as we read through these common causes please reflect upon your story and the story I shared about my own post-9/11 situation in the previous chapter. Then we'll compare notes. So here are those causes:

1. **RETIREMENT:** If you're in debt when you retire chances are good it will grow like fungus and stick around forever when your income drops to Social Security, retirement pension or investment income levels, unless you are wealthy or exceptionally well prepared. And if you don't have much or any debt when you retire you may rack it up quickly when your income drops 50% or more, which is frequently the case for retirees. I've discovered that serious debt is rampant among seniors with many of them (or you) too proud or overwhelmed to seek help.

2. **JOB LOSS OR BUSINESS FAILURE:** Whether you are innocently downsized by an economic downturn or you deserve to be fired, whether you receive a decent severance package or get kicked straight into the cold or

whether you own a business and suffer losses or have to shut it down for good, you will likely tally considerable, if not suffocating, debt.

This is true because 70% of all Americans lack the savings needed to survive even a month or two of reduced income, with almost 50% lacking enough to survive even a couple of weeks with no income. In other words, the vast majority of us live paycheck to paycheck, with consumer debt usually destroying any hope we have of actually saving money. And this was all before Covid-19.

3. **ILLNESS OR MEDICAL EMERGENCY:** As I have talked with people across America I've been shocked by how many are disabled or dealing with medical emergencies (including mental health, drugs and alcohol) or trying to recover from them, and how many of them are buried in debt. Whether it's medical debt specifically (which we'll address a little later) or just the "collateral damage" debt that accompanies health challenges, it's almost 100% likely you're struggling with debt if you've been sick or injured.

4. **DIVORCE:** Everyone knows divorce is emotionally rough on separating spouses and their families but most people don't realize its full financial impact. Gone are combined incomes and shared expenses, as most divorcees struggle to live with half the total income and twice the expense of establishing and running their own households. Add legal costs, child support, reduced productivity and emotional duress and debt becomes an all-too-frequent "given."

5. **FORCE MAJEURE (UNFORSEEABLE EVENTS):** Except for a few experts with crystal ball predictions no one sees global

pandemics like Covid-19 or Great Recessions like 2008 or even terrorist attacks like 9/11 coming, let alone a drunk or texting driver slamming into your car or a wildfire, tornado or hurricane tearing through your community.

When these unforeseen disasters strike, they tend to produce the same exact thing among victims (other than shock and devastation), which unfortunately is debt. The equation for this in my view is E=DX2, meaning emergencies (E) can take your debt (D) and double it (X2) in a heartbeat.

6. **STUDENT LOANS:** Whether you're a parent who has mortgaged your future to secure your child's (or children's) education or a college graduate who invested in your own future through student loans, you know that even with their low interest rates and flexible payment terms these loans can feel like a ball and chain attached to a lifetime sentence of hard labor. Student loans don't go away either, surviving even personal bankruptcy.

   And although most college grads and parents I've advised are keeping up with their student loans, the financial pressure often causes them to use consumer credit for other things including travel, clothing, entertainment and even basic living expenses. Meanwhile, some grads or parents who didn't qualify for federal loans have used expensive credit cards or personal loans to pay for college tuition and/or room and board at school and this debt can easily run them into the financial rocks even if they've gotten a decent job, career or income. We will look at student loan relief options in Chapter 13.

7. **BAD PLANS, HABITS AND DECISIONS:** My favorite clients start the conversation saying things like, "Hey, I made the

stupid decision to buy an expensive home (or car, motorcycle or boat) that I didn't need and couldn't afford" or "Yeah, I'm in debt because I can't stop buying things on TV (or online or at the mall)" or "I'll admit that I'm the dummy who keeps bailing my kids out of debt so now I'm knee deep in debt myself!"

I love their honesty and humility.

I've even had someone tell me, "I burned through my credit cards, my savings and even my 401K to flip a property. My plan was to make a nice profit but the market changed and now I can't sell it."

The truth is that even when we don't have hurricane force circumstances driving us into debt, we often have habits, patterns, plans or decisions that can do the same thing or worse. We will address how to deal with them as we go but this is enough for now.

YOUR STORY

You heard my story of extended unemployment and skyrocketing debt following 9/11. It involved both Force Majeure and Job Loss but it included other dynamics and lessons I'll share more about as we continue, including my lack of savings and some of my spending habits.

Now it's your turn. How did you get here and where is "here" for you?

To help you summarize your story and clarify your situation here are a few questions to answer:

1. What circumstances caused you to fall into debt?
2. What else has caused you to struggle financially?
3. Beyond the financial impact, how is debt affecting you?

4. What is your current plan to pay off your debt?
5. What kind of help or solution are you looking for?

Nice job working through these questions. I hope they helped you gain some clarity and perspective. Now let's proceed to the next chapter to learn about the four X-factor reports that can change your financial life forever.

I invite you to share your story, comments or questions regarding this chapter or other topics throughout this book with me and my team at support@Debt-FreeASAP.com. We promise to reply as quickly as possible, usually within 24 hours.

CHAPTER THREE

Your Debt Load, Net Worth, P&L & FICO

Rodney and Crystal knew they had a lot of debt but weren't sure exactly how much.

So they took turns guessing, as I listened to them talk on their speaker phone.

"I've got to have at least forty-five or fifty," said Crystal, as she tried to calculate her card balances in her head. "But I don't know how much you've got," she said to her husband.

"Well I definitely don't have as much as you!" He replied with a chortle, "But I'm guessing thirty-something, maybe forty K."

Unfortunately, neither one of them was even close.

These two clients would set one of the highest debt-load totals for non-business-related credit card debt for a couple that I've come across, with 27 accounts totaling more than $168,000, including multiple accounts with the same banks. And that didn't include their home mortgage or car loans or any kind of student loans or medical debts.

"Wow." They said at least three times each as we reviewed their long list of accounts one by one then totaled them all up. It turned out Crystal was carrying more than ninety thousand and Rodney had over $70K worth of debt.

They didn't know their total debt load and they didn't realize their monthly minimums totaled more than $4,000 a month.

"Don't worry," I consoled them. "You're not alone. Some people know their numbers to the penny, but most folks underestimate how much debt they have. They never add everything up, or they lose track or they just stop looking."

Fortunately, these two had solid incomes. But even so they were burning up most of it on minimum monthly payments and were using credit cards and falling further behind every month to keep up with their other living expenses. They were the financial equivalent of a "heart attack waiting to happen."

YOUR FOUR 'X-FACTOR' REPORTS

Welcome to your official Debt-Free Doctor's Exam. This is where you will take an honest look at your financial health and learn about four X-factors that will help you assess and improve your financial condition.

When you start a program to lose weight or lower your blood pressure, you need to collect accurate readings, whether body weight, body mass, pulse rate, systolic/diastolic readings or others. The same applies to becoming debt-free ASAP.

To get your financial recovery started we need to obtain a simple yet professional snapshot of your financial condition or baseline report. You might think of it like a preliminary X-ray or MRI or perhaps even a "before" photo to start a weight-loss program.

We will assess four critical X-factors for your success, namely your Debt Load, your Net Worth, your monthly Profit & Loss (P&L) and your FICO Score.

These assessments are basic pillars of financial management and reporting. They will serve you well not only to become debt-free but to become wealthy in time, which is our ultimate goal for you.

I wish someone had taught me about all of these valuable tools (and not just the FICO credit score) when I was younger because they naturally foster a financial mindset — and even a millionaire's mindset — that will guide your thoughts and actions toward success. So take good notes, keep them in mind and share them with others when you can.

YOUR DEBT LOAD:

If you like to make lists then you're in luck on this one, because we're simply going to list your debts. You can scribble your list on a note pad, type it up as a Word document or set it up as an Excel spreadsheet, Google doc, Apple Page or whatever format you prefer. The important thing is to organize your outstanding debts so you can see them, add them up, monitor them, update them and eliminate them ASAP!

You can include as much detail as you like but the basic info needed will look something like this:

Creditor	Balance	Minimum Pmnt	Interest%	Due Date
Capital One	2475	85	19%	20th
Home Depot	1255	47	28%	5th
Chase Slate	4723	150	23%	11th
BofA	2979	89	25%	22nd
Victoria's Secret	225	37	27%	15th
Wayfair	1772	55	27%	1st
Total	13,429	463	---	---

As you can see, this kind of simple list or dashboard provides quick and easy reference and saves you from hunting or digging to locate folded credit card statements stuffed in messy drawers, files or trash cans, or looking for long buried or deleted e-statements if you get them electronically.

You might want to organize your list alphabetically by creditor names or by highest or lowest balances, interest rates or even due dates. It all depends on your debt-elimination strategy. We'll discuss those strategies soon enough, but since I favor paying off lowest balances first to generate immediate momentum and to celebrate victories sooner than later, my list would probably look like this:

Creditor	Balance	Minimum Pmnt	Interest%	Due Date
Victoria's Secret	225	37	27%	15th
Home Depot	1255	47	28%	5th
Wayfair	1772	55	27%	1st
Capital One	2475	85	19%	20th
BofA	2979	89	25%	22nd
Chase Slate	4723	150	23%	11th
Total	13,429	490	---	---

In this case we'd whack Victoria right off the bat then go after Home Depot with a weed-whacker if not a pick-axe! You get the idea.

In addition to this list of credit card accounts, you should create another list on the same page if there's room to list other loans, whether home loans, car or truck loans or leases, boat loans, personal loans, student loans, rental property loans, whatever. The key is to gain a clear and simple overview of your debt load.

One of my great joys in life has been watching balances on these lists shrink quickly, drop steadily and then hit zero, after taking good aim and serious action toward knocking them out.

"Bam!" I've exclaimed victoriously to myself, my dogs, my wife or whoever's around more than once as I've officially paid debts down and out.

To become debt-free ASAP you need to SEE the accounts you're dealing with and keep them in your sights until they're gone. So make a list and keep it updated and visible.

YOUR NET WORTH

The next part of your financial exam is to calculate your net worth. Now if that sounds a tad bit dehumanizing, I want you to know that I think your life is priceless and that you are precious beyond any words or numbers. We're not talking about your personal value or essential worth here.

We're talking about your debt, your future wealth and your current financial condition here, so please bear with me. Your actual net worth boils down to a very simple equation:

Your Assets – Your Liabilities = Your Net Worth

Assets include anything of value that you own wholly or in part. Let's say you own a car worth $20,000 but you only owe $10,000 to pay it off. That would leave you $10,000 worth of equity or asset value to your credit. That's good! If you own a home worth $350,000 and you only owe $150,000 on it then your asset value is $200,000. That is even better.

Other examples of assets are cash in your bank account, wallet or pocket, stocks or bonds, 401K or IRA retirement funds, other properties or mineral rights, your own business or accounts receivable, your intellectual property, art, furnishings, musical instruments, computers, tech, tools or machinery.

Liabilities are just the opposite of assets. So let's say you owe $30,000 on a brand new car but can only sell it pre-owned today for $25,000. That car becomes a $5,000 liability or what dealers call "upside-down" or "underwater."

Likewise, if you owe $300,000 on a property that today would only sell for $250,000 it becomes a current liability of $50,000. Credit card debts, other loans or account payable all count as liabilities.

MAKING IT PERSONAL

So how does your net worth stack up? I know it's usually not much fun to calculate your net worth when you're struggling with debt because your net worth is usually low, zero or negative. I understand all too well!

But it still pays to run your numbers and see where you stand. In fact, let's pause here and let you do that, even if your calculations are more like rough estimates. Just tally up your major assets and liabilities the best you can.

It's important for you to pencil it out and write down an actual bottom-line number; I'll explain why in a minute. So please do your math and write down your approximate net worth before you keep reading. Go ahead and get it done!

Now, if you have a positive net worth it might create some valuable options for you when we look at your best debt solutions in coming chapters. But if your current net worth is low, zero or negative, that's okay. I've been there and I know it sucks because it shows with crystal clarity that you're upside down in debt – not a great position to be in.

But there's at least one reason why a low, zero or negative net worth can become a positive for you.

You may have noticed that when clear-cut numbers become involved in our lives, whether for measurement purposes, ratings, values or scoring...something happens. How many carats is that diamond ring? How many horsepower does that engine produce? How many miles did you walk, run or ride? How many stars did that restaurant, Amazon product or HVAC contractor receive in that customer review? And what's the exact price tag on that?

Numbers matter and they capture – and hold – our attention. It's one thing to say your finances are messed up, but it's another thing to see you have a low, zero or negative net worth in the form of an actual number! It can light a fire under your butt the way it did beneath mine not that long ago.

A FLAMING REVELATION

I've always known that "naked we come into the world and naked we go out," so I've never been preoccupied with possessions or ownership. My priorities have always been more about the adventure or shared experience of life; to enjoy the teamwork and joy of raising a family, building a successful business or a winning team. The same goes for creating something beautiful, profound or impactful for others. The high adventure and basic blessings of life have been my priorities.

But one day I took a serious look at my net worth and it revealed my financial condition in very real and unflattering terms. I didn't like my number at all! In fact it was unacceptably negative and it forced me to realize that I had tolerated it, ignored it and allowed it to not only limit me but to also limit my loved ones and perhaps even our future generations! My lousy net worth was an alarming revelation to me.

So what did I do? Did I suddenly start hustling around frantically trying to make more money? Or did I get so depressed I wanted to jump off a cliff?

No. I simply realized my thinking had been distorted for far too long and I needed to change my mind about profit, property and ownership. I basically recognized my lack of proper respect and appreciation for physical and financial assets. So I changed my mind about the subject.

I boiled my new mindset down to the following million-dollar mantra:

"I want to own, not owe."

Can you say "Amen" to that? Can you say it out loud once or twice to yourself or to your dog, cat, bird, fish or whoever else will listen? Can you repeat it ten times, a hundred times or a thousand times until it sticks in your mind, soul and spirit forever?

Oh what a difference one little letter can make in one tiny word. Wealthy people understand this difference. Millionaires appreciate and accumulate assets and they always look to increase their net worth. And so can you.

"I want to *own*, not owe!"

YOUR MONTHLY P&L

This X-factor assessment tool may strike you as the biggest "no-brainer" of all time, but for a surprisingly large number of people I've talked to it has introduced a quantum leap of personal management and organization to their lives – right up there with balancing their check books or bank accounts. (Am I talking to you?)

So what is your P&L and how should you break it down and track it?

Well, we're back to making lists. This one details your monthly income from any and all sources and your expenses from utilities and insurance payments, to rent or mortgage, to food, clothing, household items and various one-time or incidental expenses. Basically every kind of expenditure you make belongs on this monthly report.

Notice we're not calling this a budget, although it can naturally lead to one.

Your P&L is a basic management report to show the net result of your income and expenses each month, whether positive or negative and by how much.

As you study your P&L you will naturally see areas or line items to cut, reduce, limit or manage better in some way. For instance, you might notice that your electric bill spikes in the summer from running your air conditioning, so you can plan ahead (budget) to either cut some other summer costs or to direct additional income toward that bill to help compensate. You might also notice random fees for services you don't need, use or want and decide to reduce or eliminate those.

The goal is to operate with a positive or profitable monthly cash flow that produces a surplus and avoid the opposite scenario that drags you further into debt.

If you make cuts and still have a negative cash flow, you'll need to look for ways to add income, sell assets or reduce your debt load ASAP.

Without showing every line item, here's a basic P&L outline by category:

PROFIT/INCOME:

Source #1

Source #2

Source #3

LOSS/EXPENSE:

Giving/Charitable

Savings/Retirement

Rent/Mortgage

Vehicles (loans, leases, maintenance, gas)

Utilities

Insurance

Food/Household

Clothing

Personal Loans

Credit Cards

Taxes

Travel/Special

Miscellaneous

Once you start paying closer attention to your monthly income and expenses and actually SEE the numbers and TRACK where your money is going by category you will start making smarter financial decisions and living a healthier financial lifestyle. It's only natural to be more careful with your finances when you pay closer attention to them. So watch your P&L!

YOUR FICO SCORE

Last but not least among your financial X-factors is your FICO credit score. This one should come as no surprise, since most of us know the importance of our credit reports. I can share a few insider facts you might want to know, but let's review the basics first.

The FICO score was established in 1989 by the Fair Isaac Corporation, a consumer analytics software company, to help lenders assess risk for lending money to various borrowers, based on their financial histories.

A FICO score basically estimates your creditworthiness and is derived by blending and analyzing information from three leading credit bureaus that track the credit-related activities of consumers, namely Transunion, Experian and Equifax.

FICO scores range from 350 to 850. Scores falling within the 670 to 740 range are considered "good" by most lenders. Lower scores are considered "fair" or "poor" while higher ones are "very good" or "excellent" depending on where they land.

What criteria are used to determine your score? There are five main categories, each one weighted by a certain percentage of the total score, as follows:

FICO SCORE CRITERIA:

35% - Payment History

30% - Outstanding Debt/Debt Usage

15% - Account Age

10% - Credit Mix

10% - New Credit/Inquiries

You can learn more about the fine points of this scoring system through some easy online research, but here are your main take-away notes to remember:

1. Late payments are deadly.
2. High debt loads or maxed accounts are also seriously negative.
3. Credit accounts held for years show good responsibility.
4. A mixture of installment loans and credit cards is desirable.

5. New accounts and "hard" credit inquiries (when creditors pull your FICO report to approve or decline your application) can ding your score.

We will talk more about your FICO score as we discuss your debt-relief options in the chapters ahead, since your score will either dictate which options are most attractive (or available) to you or your score will be affected in some way by the option you choose.

GETTING YOUR SCORE & INSIDER TIPS

If you don't know your current credit score, I encourage you to set up a free and secure account on CreditKarma.com. It won't provide your exact FICO score but it will allow you to track all your credit accounts in real time and get pretty good ballpark credit scores from two of the three FICO reporting bureaus, Equifax and Transunion, without any negative impact on your credit. Your access is 24/7.

Or you can request a confidential copy of your credit report once a year for free without negatively impacting your credit. Just go to annualcreditreport.com or call 1-877-322-8228. You can also complete the Annual Credit Report Request Form and mail it to: Annual Credit Report Request Service, P.O. Box 105281, Atlanta GA 30348-5281 if you prefer.

As for other insider "secrets," here are a few.

The first one you should know is that there are *numerous versions* of FICO reports, including several different ones used by mortgage lenders, auto lenders and other creditors. This means your normal everyday FICO score (usually the FICO 8 version) isn't necessarily the same one your lenders will use. Their versions weigh certain factors more heavily than others, sometimes making your score lower on their report, which can be upsetting to discover when you're trying to qualify for a home or car loan or get the best interest rates. Sometimes it will pay to check your FICO score from these specialized versions before making a major purchase. They're available online or you can contact us for assistance via our email address at the end of this chapter.

Another little-known fact is that FICO isn't the only player in the credit score game. Perhaps you've heard of the Vantage credit score? It's one of several slightly different scoring systems based on their own algorithms used by some creditors, but not by most. FICO is still king of the credit scoring world, so don't be confused or misled by other credit scores you might encounter.

Another insider fact pertains to paying off your debts and accidentally hurting your FICO score in the process. How can that happen? It can happen one of two ways.

The first way is if you pay off an installment loan. Let's say you have a $20,000 car loan paid down to a balance of just $1,000. This looks great for your credit profile because your account shows a very low balance with a whopping $19,000 of unused or "available" credit. That's a huge positive.

But as soon as you pay off that last $1,000 balance, the account will close and remove the entire $20,000 of unused credit from your credit profile, thus adjusting your overall credit usage rate downward and creating negative impact on your FICO score just when you thought that getting rid of a big debt would be a big victory!

Fortunately, the negative effect should be just temporary as the successfully paid-off loan is ultimately viewed as a positive development, with some scoring adjustments to follow. Just be careful if you're planning a major credit-sensitive purchase (like buying a house or refinancing), as you might want to slow down paying off an installment loan when that balance is getting low and the available credit limit is high and helping your score.

The second way to hurt your score by paying off a debt isn't so forgiving. In this case let's imagine you pay off a revolving credit card account with a $5,000 credit limit. That's great! But rather than leave it at zero balance and allow your $5,000 of available credit to boost your overall credit usage rate and FICO score, let's say you go ahead and close that account.

This is a no-no, unless you want to *lower* your credit score! That's because $5,000 of unused credit sitting on your credit report is sexy stuff to the FICO scoring formulas and is sorely missed if it's gone! Losing that account's history or "age" will also lower the average age of all your accounts and hurt your overall credit profile as a result.

I've made this mistake myself and I've talked with many others who have zealously paid off debts and closed those accounts to "get rid of them once and for all," without understanding the impact to their FICO score.

So now you know better. Chopping up your credit cards is fine to avoid using them, but closing your accounts can be harmful to your financial health.

ONE MORE FICO TIP

My last FICO-related insider tip relates to important debt-balance thresholds or benchmarks you should be aware of.

To simplify this one, let's say you've got a $2,600 balance on a credit card with a $5,000 credit limit. This equates to a 52% utilization rate, which is healthy and fine and certainly better than if your balance was $4,600 or a 92% usage rate.

As we noted earlier FICO scoring involves algorithms that penalize high balances, especially balances over 75% of the credit limit and of course even more so those over 90%, while rewarding lower balances, especially when they're under 50%, 30% or best of all, under 10%.

Going back to our example, you should gain a significant boost to your FICO score just by paying your balance down from $2,600 to something under $2,500, to drop that utilization rate below the 50% threshold.

The disclaimer here is that FICO scoring is complex, mysterious and all-encompassing, so lowering one account balance below a significant threshold should help but it won't necessarily do so if other account balances are fluctuating or suddenly spiking. The FICO scoring system is holistic, just as our debt-conquering approach should be.

With that said, I've carefully monitored the kind of FICO-boosting moves we're discussing here and have seen consistent results. So keep an eye on your debt utilization rates and be aggressive whenever you can but especially when you see your debt balances hovering slightly above 90%, 75%, 50%, 30% or 10% thresholds. When you see them there, go ahead and boost your score by paying them down if you can. And if you're in doubt, blast away at your debt, anyway! It's hard to go wrong paying down debt.

YOUR FINANCIAL IQ

I can't promise you'll start reading the *Wall Street Journal* with breakfast every morning just because you read this chapter, but I can guarantee that your financial IQ will rise as you manage your finances by tracking your Debt Load, calculating your Net Worth, managing your P&L and improving your FICO.

And please don't be discouraged if you're slightly overwhelmed.

Take a deep breath and remember these tools are simple; simple lists, simple math, simple tracking and simply paying attention.

And here's a nice little bonus to keep in mind. Just by using these tools you will join the exclusive ranks of the world's best financial experts, top business leaders and most successful millionaires and billionaires - and that's pretty sexy.

To help you organize, assess and manage your finances we have created special X-factor forms you can receive free at Debt-FreeASAP.com. You will find them atop our Products & Programs page.

CHAPTER FOUR

Your Mindset, Spirit & Vision

"I am so embarrassed to be making this call," said Cindy, a thirty-something professional from the San Francisco Bay area. "This is so embarrassing," she added.

"Well, I totally understand," I said, almost like a funeral director or confessional priest, then added more brightly, 'Debt really sucks!"

Thankfully she laughed. And I could hear some of the shame and self-condemnation lift off her, at least for a moment.

I can't remember how much debt Cindy owed or what circumstances got her into trouble but I do remember telling her the same thing I tell people every day.

"Here's the truth," I said. "Most people struggling with debt didn't go on wild shopping sprees or exotic vacations. Most have been solid citizens who've paid their bills and tried to manage their money – until something happened."

"Right," she said, halfway convinced.

"That's the truth," I said matter-of-factly.

"Right," she repeated, now maybe 75% convinced.

"It doesn't take much of an emergency or setback for people to rack up $20,000 to $30,000 of debt these days and then all bets are off," I continued. "It can get real ugly real fast."

"Tell me about it," she said knowingly.

"But you know what changes everything?" I asked her.

"No, what's that?"

"What you decide to do about it." I said point blank. "How you respond, to get help, to create a plan, to take action."

"Right, I get it," she said as her embarrassment evaporated and her mindset started to shift.

YOUR MINDSET

Your mind is a battlefield.

Life is great or it's your worst day ever. You're Einstein smart or the dumbest person in the world. You're 100% right or you're absolutely wrong. You're stuck in debt and so embarrassed! It all depends on your state of mind.

If you read Chapter One you know how I thought and felt about being in debt. It hammered my self-esteem every day and tormented my mind every night. It took just six months for me to go from brilliant high-flying executive pitching big-time deals to Fortune 500 clients to grounded, depressed, indecisive and debt-riddled guy with no job, no direction and no financial destiny in mind.

Your mind is also a powerful machine.

What your mind wants and needs is clarity, direction, and a destination. We crave answers, options and solutions. Our minds want to make decisions, to be resolute, to take decisive action toward our best and smartest outcomes. Your decision to read or listen to this book is a healthy start. But prepare your mind to make bigger and bolder decisions that will determine your financial destiny.

I've seen the power of changing your mind or making a decision, and I'm guessing you have too.

For me it was at the age of 16, when I crashed into a house on Halloween night during a car chase with police. I got thrown in jail and kicked off my high school football team. Thankfully no one got hurt, but I was totally devastated and realized I was just a dumb jock with no direction. So I dug deep and decided to change my mind and change my direction.

I decided to hit the books, hit the weights, hit the sprints, hills and stairs – and even hit opposing football players – like never before.

Despite my huge set-back and modest mental and physical abilities I was determined to make it to a good college and maybe even to play pro football someday, no matter how far-fetched such dreams looked at the time.

Thanks to my new mindset, direction and actions, everything changed so dramatically that just one year later I was being recruited by Harvard and Brown universities and was playing pro football just a handful of years later.

In similar fashion my debt recovery started when I decided to face the problem and deal with it decisively. I didn't know all my options the way you will in the next section of this book, but at least I decided to take action. And I believe you will, too.

Most people struggle to change their minds. They're stubborn and insecure. They're stuck in their ways and are afraid to admit they're wrong or need help or need to find a better way. But not you.

How do I know this?

Because you're here right now. You've already recognized your need and decided to take action. You've come this far and your mind is set on breaking free from the slavery of debt and you won't let anything keep you in chains. Your mind is set on finding a new path toward wealth and opportunity.

We will study a number of possible paths in just a moment, including several I have utilized myself over the years.

But first let's get spiritual for a minute.

YOUR SPIRIT

God knows how badly debt can oppress our souls, grieve our spirits and negatively impact whole generations.

If you skipped over my short Dedication page story about my grandfather and his massive debt back in the Great Depression, please flip back there and read it now.

Debt destroyed his marriage, disbanded his family and stole a relationship that I miss dearly to this day. My grandfather was a Greek immigrant who became an exceptional real estate developer in Chicago. Yet I only met him a couple times and never got to know him or learn about his (or my) extended family or Greek heritage. If only I could have spent more time around him and his beautiful mansion in the great city of Chicago! (Although I must admit growing up on sunny SoCal beaches wasn't all bad.)

The long-term spiritual effects of debt have been known for thousands of years. In the Bible's book of Leviticus God commanded the children of Israel to celebrate a Year of Jubilee every 50 years. During that year, all debts were to be forgiven, all slaves, prisoners and servants released and all properties returned to their original owners while everyone experienced mercy and restoration.

Can you imagine that kind of joyful celebration?

This spiritual law speaks to the bondage, discouragement and inequality debt can create in our communities and in our spirits. It also speaks to the supernatural importance of breaking the otherwise endless cycle of debt, poverty and bondage, and to the supernatural joy it releases in our hearts to become debt-free.

This echoes some of what Harv Eker wrote about breaking free from distorted financial "blueprints" in his book that I cited in this book's Introduction.

So whether you are spiritually minded or not I encourage you to exercise whatever faith you can muster to call out for supernatural grace, mercy, wisdom and deliverance from any false beliefs, misconceptions or any other forms of bondage or poverty that debt can produce in your spirit and in your finances. Go ahead and give it a try, it doesn't hurt to ask.

True spirituality breaks chains and sets us free from bondage and fear. Jesus said that nothing is too difficult for our heavenly father who rewards all who seek him by faith and that even a tiny mustard seed of faith can move mountains. So feel free to pray for your mountain of debt to be removed and I will join you!

And one final thought. If you've ever cursed yourself by saying "I'm *always* in debt," or "I'll *never* get out of debt," or you believe that you're somehow doomed to be in debt or financial distress because of your family background or some other circumstance that seems unshakable then I exhort you to change that belief. This is what the old-time word "repent" actually means.

In this case it means you admit you are wrong to make sweeping generalizations or to judge or curse yourself (or others) harshly as it relates to finances and you seek supernatural power to renew your mind and spirit, instead. That's a prayer I've never seen denied.

YOUR VISION

"Where there is no vision, the people perish," says one of my favorite proverbs. What does it mean?

It means we need vision! (And by "we" I mean you.)

Goals are great, plans are important, but vision is divine because it draws us upward and onward – almost magically and magnetically – toward our destination or destiny. And vision naturally produces goals and plans to get there.

Vision is your ability to see the future with imagination.

You might want to read that sentence again and maybe even say it out loud to yourself once or twice to make sure it sticks, as you imagine a debt-free future.

President John F. Kennedy had a vision to put a man on the moon. His vision produced an audacious goal to make it happen before 1970 which in turn produced the plans to get there step-by-step, and finally with "a giant leap for mankind."

Mother Teresa had a vision to care for the poorest of the poor around the world, Martin Luther King Jr. had a dream (or vision) for racial justice and equality, Walt Disney had a vision for a Magic Kingdom full of colorful characters, rides and stories, Steve Jobs had a vision for user-friendly technology with style and Elon Musk had (and still has) a vision for electric cars, underground transport and space travel to Mars.

Vision is exciting! And vision naturally attracts *provision*, whether from customers, donors, investors, employers, friends, family members or even strangers.

Some say this provision manifests from The Universe through quantum physics, but I believe it flows from the Creator of the Universe. Either way there seems to be a supernatural dynamic or "law of attraction" that draws provision toward vision like bees to honey or moths to the light.

I've seen these dynamics unleashed on numerous occasions, perhaps most notably when I moved to Dallas ahead of my family in 2004 to partner with a friend to build his real estate business. I was still recovering from debt and was still broke and living with my friend and his family in their spare bedroom, while just starting to earn a solid income.

Our company bought and sold homes all over Dallas-Fort Worth, so I got to visit and evaluate neighborhoods everywhere with an eye toward moving and settling my family as soon as possible, in the nicest area possible.

One day I discovered an area in the city of McKinney called Eldorado.

At the time I didn't know that name referred to a mythical sixteenth century "city of gold" featuring fabulous wealth and opportunity somewhere in the jungles of South America but I thought this Eldorado was pretty special in its own right.

This Eldorado featured gentle hills, soaring trees, pretty trails and custom homes that would cost millions of dollars in LA (or even in Dallas' fancier neighborhoods) but were far less in this suburb.

There was even one castle-like home with heavy wood doors, stone and ironwork imported from England by the creators of the long-running children's hit show *Barney & Friends* who had built that home near a beautiful lake where I pulled over to stop and feast my eyes.

That is where I caught a vision that both stirred my faith and challenged it.

My vision was to live in this area ASAP despite the fact I had no money and couldn't qualify for any loan, let alone one for homes like these. I knew I was crazy to consider such thoughts as I sat in my car admiring the manicured paths, homes and grounds around the lake and the fountain spraying high in the middle of it.

But my vision was set.

Later that same day as I cruised the neighborhood, I spotted a stately corner home near a prize winning elementary school just down the street from the local country club. It reminded me of my grandfather's historic home in Chicago and it had a For Sale or Lease sign out front. And it was love at first sight.

Vision produces a make-it-happen attitude no matter what the obstacles.

In this case I called the number on the sign and quickly met and befriended the owner, shared my vision and negotiated a discounted lease agreement that allowed me and my family to move in right away. We later bought the home within just a year, thanks to the amazing provision that poured in as I helped build our fast-growing company.

I had come to Dallas broke, broken and without vision. But I came to join and support my friend's vision – and perhaps borrow some of its power – and that led me to that lake and to a vision of my own.

Vision is contagious.

Vision attracts people, provision and naturally produces goals and plans to make it all happen. A mustard seed of faith can move mountains. And nothing is impossible for those who believe.

Can you see your future with imagination? Can you envision yourself debt-free and even wealthy, whatever that looks like to you? I hope that you can because we're heading that way. So grab your new mindset, your renewed spirit and your fresh vision and let's take a look at your options!

PART II
YOUR OPTIONS

CHAPTER FIVE

The Hi-Low Payoff Plan

"Hey man," said Brandon, a casual mid-twenties caller who jumped straight to his point. "I've heard you're supposed to pick either your biggest debt or your smallest one to pay off first...can you tell me the deal on that?"

"Sure, I can break it down for you," I said with a chuckle. "Where did you hear about this approach?"

"A friend of mine told me his dad or grandpa or someone he knows recommended it. But he forgot exactly how it works," he said.

"No problem," I replied. "I call it the old-school Hi-Low Payoff Plan and it's a classic!"

"Okay, cool!" He said with his own chuckle.

PICK YOUR POISON, BUT IN A GOOD WAY

Debt is like financial poison. We know that. The question here is how you want to get rid of it, strategically speaking. And by that I mean following a systematic plan, in this case to invest your money toward paying off certain target debts or a specific group of high-priority accounts, whether the highest or lowest balances or the highest interest rates first, ahead of other accounts you handle like usual in the meantime.

There are two main variables to consider. The first one is your account balances, whether you target the highest or lowest ones first, and the second is each account's interest rate.

In Chapter Three, I mentioned my preference for paying off low balance accounts first, but let's review why I said that. It's a no-brainer to me because your smaller account balances are closer to zero and therefore easiest for you to pay off quickly so you can yell "Bam!" to yourself or to whoever's around or to bust out your debt-free happy dance when you zero out an account.

This approach creates momentum, highlights your progress and releases endorphins throughout your body as you celebrate victory and success; a valuable and powerful combination when you're digging out of a financial hole, changing your habits and transforming your future.

This approach also offers the benefit of eliminating at least one monthly payment whenever you zero out an account, which frees up extra cash flow to pay off other debts more aggressively. So if your Anthropology card balance is $450 and your Home Depot account is $750, go ahead and knock that Anthropology card out pronto! Then take whatever that monthly payment was, plus anything else you can scrape together to add to it, and blast away at Home Depot.

And once that one's gone you move on to the next lowest balance.

This approach is a winner but there are still some who prefer to take aim at their biggest debt first, especially if it's chained to a high interest rate or has some other consideration.

EXCEPTIONS & VARIABLES

One exception to the "lowest first" rule would be to keep an eye out for large installment loans (such as a car, appliance, home or personal) which have the same relatively large payment amount each month for the full term of the loan or other financing.

Because as soon as their balances drop into the vicinity of other accounts you are targeting, they make good sense to tackle quickly and here's why.

Let's say your lowest debt balance and next target account to eliminate is a $900 Macy's card with 27% interest and a $45/month payment. Now imagine your next highest balance is $1,200 on a GM truck loan at 7.5% interest and a monthly payment of $500/month. Which should you attack first?

Hopefully you're thinking GM even though it's not your lowest balance yet. The reason is that even though it's a slightly higher balance than Macy's you will save a whopping $500 monthly payment as soon as you pay it off. This makes more sense than just eliminating Macy's $900 balance and $45 monthly payment, right? By eliminating the larger GM payment, you would free up $500 a month to help you chop down other debts (including Macy's) in dramatic fashion. That's a pretty smart move.

Another exception to the "lowest first" rule would be when you have multiple balances in the same ball park, and one of them has a significantly higher interest rate. This speaks to the second variable of the Hi-Low Payoff Plan; the interest rate.

Let's imagine you have two similar debts, a Chase card balance of $1,700 and a Wells Fargo card of $1,500. If you blindly follow the 'lowest first' approach you would attack the smaller Wells Fargo balance before going after the Chase card. But what would happen if the larger Chase card's interest rate was 27% and the Wells Fargo was a special 9.9% promotional rate?

In this case it would make sense to pivot and pay off the larger Chase balance first because its high interest rate is burning up more of your money every month than the Wells account is. So you could go ahead and pay off the higher interest Chase account ahead of the smaller debt if you wanted to make that exception.

PAY THEM OFF...BUT DON'T CLOSE 'EM!

One word of caution I will repeat from our earlier FICO discussion. When you successfully pay a credit card balance down to zero do NOT close that account, unless you don't mind taking a hit to your credit score.

Why is that? Because closing a zero balance account can actually lower your score. How? By removing a credit line that has a certain amount of "age" it will impact FICO scoring formulas that reward you for managing credit accounts over a period of years.

You will also remove precious "available credit" from your credit score calculation if you close the account by removing that account's credit limit, which will then reduce your overall amount of available credit and thus negatively impact your overall profile. You can review FICO scoring in Chapter Three if you need a refresh.

SUMMARY:

The Option: Hi-Low Payoff Plan

The Concept: Target certain debts to pay off first, whether highest interest or lowest balances, using extra funds whenever possible.

Best Benefit: Simple, organized approach to eliminate debt and raise financial IQ.

Best Suited: Any time you're capable of making regular and even additional payments to reduce debt balances.

FICO Effect: This approach leads to steady FICO score improvement.

Other Notes: Some people make extra payments on their targeted debts each month to reduce their principal balance faster, whether by doubling or tripling their minimum payments or by making additional payments on targeted accounts every time they get paid (if more than once a month), or by using "side hustle" income, bonuses, gifts or tax return funds to make it happen.

CHAPTER SIX

Debt Consolidation

"Hey, how do you feel about debt consolidation?" My friend Bob asked as we walked to our cars after a social event, attempting to keep our conversation casual. Of course I knew this wasn't exactly small-talk.

Bob knew about my work and had previously told me his wife's job had been downsized so I knew he was dealing with financial distress.

"It can be a good option," I said. "But there are two or three types with different requirements, so it depends on your situation," I added.

"Oh." He sounded discouraged to hear it might be complicated.

"But don't worry," I assured him. "Chances are good that one of the options can work for you."

"That's good," he said, apparently interested to hear more.

"Look," I continued. "We can take a minute to cover the highlights now or we can get together another time to look at your big picture and review all your options."

"It's up to you," I added.

"Let's definitely get together on the big picture," he said, "but I would love a quick summary now if you don't mind."

"No problem," I said as I motioned toward his car and we continued walking. "I'll give you my quick ABC's of Debt

Consolidation," I told him, as I shared an abbreviated version of what follows here.

A. PERSONAL OR HOME EQUITY LOAN

In a perfect world, Bob would secure a low-interest loan of $25,000 or whatever amount he needed to pay off a bunch (or all) of his high-interest credit cards or other bothersome debts totaling that same amount. That is classic debt-consolidation.

You get one low interest loan to pay off multiple high interest debts.

This approach would save him a boatload of interest expense and lower his monthly payment, sometimes dramatically. This in turn would reduce his financial stress, improve his P&L and better manage his debt load, so long as he didn't turn around and run up his old (consolidated) credit cards again.

The challenge here is to get that low-interest loan of $25,000 – or whatever amount is needed.

This is where the old adage is so unfortunately true; "Banks are happy to lend you money when you don't need it, but not interested when you do!"

Even if you have significant equity in your home, borrowing against it will require a certain FICO score, employment/income record and attractive debt-to-income ratio on your monthly P&L.

To make matters worse, many banks will look at you a little cross-eyed if they see you've piled up a bunch of high interest debt, and may not be crazy about handing you a fresh stack of cash, as a result!

If you do qualify and can consolidate your debt with a low interest home loan they're a great way to go, whether as part of a Cash-out Refinance or a Home Equity Line of Credit (HELOC) or some other arrangement. The lower interest rates and other favorable terms of these loans (such as stretching your payments over numerous years through amortization) can dramatically lower your payments and create serious relief.

Shifting high interest credit card or other debt into a home-based consolidation loan can also make your interest payments tax deductible (because interest on home loans is tax deductible), which can also be another nice benefit for you. Just be sure to check your situation with an accountant.

With that said there are some financial experts who advise against using home equity to deal with consumer debt for fear of jeopardizing your most valuable (secured) asset by attaching unsecured debt to it. They make a good point, but in most cases, people struggling with debt don't have any better alternatives.

Whatever the case, be clear about your loan's terms, especially the cost of originating the loan, and be sure to check with your accountant about any tax implications or other ramifications that might come with the loan.

The same basic dynamics apply to personal loans from banks, credit unions or online lenders, except for the potential tax benefits, which only apply to home loans.

When seeking consolidation loans always be careful to evaluate the interest rate you are offered because in some cases you CAN get a loan but the interest rate is as high as or even higher than the credit cards or other debts you're already struggling with. You don't want to add fuel to your already flaming finances by adding more high-interest debt!

The unfortunate temptation (or sadly frequent pattern) in the debt-consolidation loan scenario is to get a new consolidation loan or credit line to help alleviate your immediate financial distress, but then forget to pay off your existing debts with the new money and wind up with double your debt load and twice your monthly overhead! That turns an "A-grade" debt consolidation plan into an "F."

B – BALANCE TRANSFER CARDS

Imagine you're shipwrecked on a pile of high interest debt in the middle of a perilous financial ocean and along comes a life-saving 0% balance transfer card to your rescue. What do you do? Of course you jump on board and transfer as much high interest debt as you can, from as many accounts as you can!

This is another way you can consolidate high interest credit card debt.

I have spoken with hundreds of people who have used balance transfer cards and some of them live to tell a story with good results and a happy ending. They were able to aggressively pay down their entire debt during their typical 12 to 18 month promotional period without jumping (or falling) back into the shark-infested waters by accumulating other debt on other cards.

The truth is 0% balance transfer cards can offer massive relief to weary debtors who qualify for them. Using them can be a smart move. Qualifying for them is usually the challenge no matter how "Pre-Approved" the letter or email says that you are. Balance transfer card approvals require pretty good FICO scores and income levels.

It's important to note that these cards also work out well for banks as they "hook" well qualified high-balance debtors (aka "whales") and often keep them hooked for years at high interest rates once their promotional rates expire and their normal high rate kicks back in for the long haul.

The banks know from years of experience that most debtors won't pay off their transferred balances during the promotional period. And most of the transfer card debtors I've spoken with have gotten hooked in this manner, so you have to be aware of that and take full advantage of the zero interest rate to pay your debt load off while you can.

C – DEBT-CONSOLIDATION PROGRAMS

If you don't qualify for consolidation loans or balance transfer cards but you still want to consolidate your debts into one lower monthly payment, you might want to consider a debt consolidation or "debt management" program offered by a variety of companies and non-profit organizations.

Once you sign up with one of these groups they will contact your creditors to negotiate a reduced interest rate and lower payment for you while committing to manage your payments for you.

Each month you will make just one payment to your consolidator and they will disburse those funds to all your participating creditors as agreed. Please note the word "participating" because not all creditors will play along – sometimes because you don't yet qualify for a program in their eyes or because they don't work with your consolidation company. Just be sure to check if your consolidator can work with all your targeted creditors.

The consolidation group will typically charge you a monthly management fee and they frequently collect fees from the creditors as well.

Are there any qualifications for these programs? Yes.

In most cases creditors will not negotiate lower interest or payment terms with your consolidator unless you are already 2 to 3 months behind on your payments and are dealing with a legitimate hardship situation. If you don't meet these criteria your creditors will expect you to make your normal payments to stay current and would have no need, urgency or motivation to discount your payment terms.

If you're wondering how this kind of program affects your FICO score then you understand the Catch-22 of debt-consolidation/management programs!

THE CATCH-22 & COLD REALITY

Banks are not charitable organizations. They rarely help customers unless those customers have faced or are facing calamities that jeopardize the collection of their principle and interest. And even then it's done grudgingly.

In fact I have spoken with literally dozens of hurricane, heart attack or other legitimate victims who swear they have begged their creditors for help but gotten no relief *because their payments were current*. In other words, since their accounts posed no threat of loss or collection expense to the creditor, the creditor had no need or motivation to help.

Thankfully the Covid-19 Pandemic has prompted many banks and other creditors to offer a variety of helpful options. We will discuss them further next chapter.

But let's go back to the Catch-22 of debt consolidation, before we jump ahead. As I mentioned your accounts have to be in distress from missed or late payments to qualify. And the creditor will usually close your account in the process, meaning you can no longer use it and it will not reopen when you pay it off.

Both of these factors create a negative impact on your FICO score, leading to a tough decision for many people.

Do they care more about following a consolidated debt reduction plan and getting relief? Or would they rather scratch and claw to maintain whatever FICO score they currently have, without getting reduced interest or monthly payments?

And here again, when I say 'they' I mean you.

In most cases your answer depends on variables unique to your situation. Such variables can include your future prospects, employment or health status, pending transactions, expenses, etc.

Such questions beg for careful consideration and often for some friendly counsel from a trusted accountant, coach, advisor or financially savvy family member.

SUMMARY:

The Option: Debt Consolidation

The Concept: Reduce your interest, monthly payment and debt load faster by transferring debt to lower interest loans, cards or consolidation programs.

Best Benefit: Lowers your monthly overhead and simplifies your financial plan.

FICO Effect: Consolidation loans or transfer cards will usually boost your score by clearing previously maxed accounts and opening a new account, while debt-consolidation/management programs will lower your score (if it's not already distressed) by closing your accounts.

Best Suited: Consolidation loans and transfer cards are best for qualified but over-extended debtors. Debt-consolidation/management programs are best for debtors in significant distress.

Other Notes: Be careful not to rack up new debt on old accounts after consolidating them elsewhere!

CHAPTER SEVEN

Hardship Payment Plans

"So, what do you think I should do?" asked the stressed out single mother named Angie, over the phone.

We had just done a panoramic review of her credit card accounts, most of which were running a month or two behind, thanks to a nasty breakup with her boyfriend. And her disability and part-time work income was limited.

"Have you talked to your creditors?" I asked.

"Hell no!" she growled. "I tried to tell them what's going on but they were pushy and rude and they refuse to stop calling. So now I leave my ringer off or only answer calls I recognize. Wish I could hunt 'em down and hit 'em with a skillet!"

"Yeah," I said, laughing at her thought. "You're in a tough time-frame for collection calls," I said. "They go nuts as soon as you fall behind."

"They sure as hell do," she concurred.

"Well, you're going to have to ignore them a little longer," I advised her. "Then you're going to call them up and tell them what I tell you to say."

"I am?" She wondered, skeptically.

"Yup," I assured her. "Then you're going to call me up and tell me how smart and wonderful I am!" I joked and she laughed till she was coughing.

A BETTER-KNOWN SECRET

Millions of Americans have come to learn about hardship payment programs offered by creditors due to the disastrous effects of the Covid-19 pandemic. During this crisis many banks and other creditors have graciously and proactively sought to help customers struggling to keep up, through a variety of hardship programs reducing or suspending payments or fees (which used to be kept relatively secret), including the federal government's CARES Act, which allows many homeowners to reduce or defer their mortgage payments for up to 12 months if they've been financially affected.

I'll discuss that program further in Chapter Thirteen as well as Coronavirus-related (and ongoing) student loan relief programs.

Prior to this emergency situation (when I spoke with Angie) and probably after things return to "normal" these programs will retreat back into the shadows and into relative secrecy.

So I will share with you what I told Angie and others with similar situations about how hardship programs work and how to participate in them. And it's really quite simple.

Banks and other creditors have learned that when it comes to debtors in distress it's better to smile, offer some help and collect *some* money through a special payment plan than it is to stay hostile and get nothing.

But they usually won't smile right away.

The key for lenders is timing, so they won't offer help until they're sure you need it (or until they're facing serious odds of losing money), usually after 2 to 3 missed payments. Until that time, they're in full collection mode with endless collection calls and questions like "So how much can you pay today?" or "When can I schedule your next payment?" (I'll discuss stopping these calls in Chapter Thirteen as well.)

Once Angie, you or anyone else falls 2 to 3 payments behind, the bank has a serious decision to make. Do they keep up with their bothersome collection efforts? Do they turn your account over to a bulldog collection company and let them give it their best shot? Do they charge your account off as a loss for tax purposes, and then sell what's left of it to a wholesale collection company? Or do they try to reach you with a special offer?

A TIME TO TALK

This is when you want to contact them. And when you do, you don't want to speak with normal customer service agents, in most cases. Such agents will typically just pull your account up and wear you down with the same old scripted questions about catching up on missed payments or resuming normal payments.

So what do you do? You tell them you need to speak with someone handling their hardship payment program.

Once you reach someone in that department, you can explain your situation and answer a few questions, now easier softballs like, "Do you know how much you can afford each month?" and then listen to what they can offer.

They will usually offer to reduce your interest rate dramatically, sometimes all the way down to 7% or even 0% in some cases and cancel some or all your late fees. They will then reduce your monthly payment amount to a flat and affordable figure that you'll pay (automatically as a bank debit) every month until the balance is eliminated.

Your account will normally be frozen or closed by this point due to your missed payments, but now it will be officially closed. That's just part of the deal, right along with halting any further collection calls or fees.

Just remember this is a hardship plan designed to relieve your financial pressure and avoid further distress. It is not a credit repair program. That will come later once you stabilize your situation and gradually recover.

WORTH THE EFFORT

Making these calls and having these conversations with creditors is not easy if you are busy, sick or overwhelmed by work, kids, relationship stress or even the thought of making outbound phone calls. It's especially challenging if you have a good number of creditors to call.

But you can do it.

To make hardship payment arrangements and successfully follow through on them requires some simple organization and effort. You will need to schedule some time to make calls, whether one at a time if your time is limited or multiple calls if you can block out more time.

You will need to list your accounts and take and keep notes for each conversation. And you should definitely create a file, either a physical or digital file to keep your notes and relevant documents (agreement letters, statements, etc.) from each conversation.

You will feel great every time you make these payment arrangements because instead of dodging collection calls and suffering duress or hiding in the darkness of an uncertain future you are being proactive, honest, up-front and resolute about dealing with your debt in a respectful and honorable way.

SUMMARY:

The Option: Hardship Payment Programs

The Concept: Create a payment plan with discounted terms directly with creditors after falling behind on payments.

Best Benefit: Dramatically reduce interest rate and monthly payment amount.

FICO Effect: Initially negative due to late payments and account closures but gradually positive as account balances get paid off over time.

Best Suited: For hardship situations with missed payments and already damaged FICO score.

Other Notes: Remember not to contact creditors until you've missed at least two payments. If you accidentally answer a collection call before then just politely state that you are dealing with a hardship situation and will be in touch as soon as you can. If they offer to connect you with someone in the hardship program or department or are authorized to offer you an immediate hardship plan, then remain polite and hear them out and move forward if their offer is acceptable. Otherwise be polite, hang up, stay positive and stick with your plan.

CHAPTER EIGHT

Family Assistance

"I've got to do something about my debt," said Katie, a 36-year old marketing professional. "I'm even thinking about asking my parents for help," she added, like that was her worst-case scenario.

"Okay," I said.

"Isn't that pathetic?" she said, more a self-condemnation than a question. "I mean, what do you think about that?"

"Well, it depends on a bunch of things," I told her. "Like how much debt you have, how much they've helped you in the past, and of course their overall financial situation. Yours, too," I added. "It's hard to say without knowing more."

"Yeah," she said, distracted by her own thoughts.

"Look," I said. "These situations can be complicated and messy, or they can be no big deal, it depends on the circumstances."

"Uh huh."

"So let's look at your situation," I continued. "And as we review your options, I can share some guidelines, ground rules and suggestions about getting help from your family as we go. Then you can pick your best approach."

"How does that sound?" I asked her.

"Perfect." she said, and we continued from there.

WHY AGE MATTERS

The first thing I told Katie was that getting help from family members is very common, with probably 20% of my younger clients ultimately opting for this approach. It seems to happen naturally when they discuss their options and plans with their trusted family members, who in turn offer to help in some way.

This is especially true when there are no-fault disasters like Covid-19 ravaging the economy and forcing family members to seek (or offer) help in extraordinary ways.

In more ordinary times and situations however, age seems to matter.

There seems to be an unwritten rule in our modern-day culture that getting financial help from your family is totally cool, as long as you're under 30. There are several reasons for this including the fact that our twenties are often filled with trial and error, adventure, student loans and growing pains that can require family assistance. And most parents (or other family members) are agreeable and forgiving, at least to a point. Most parents are also in their prime earning years, typically in their 40s or 50s, which certainly helps.

There is no rule, however, against seeking or receiving help whether straight bail-out gifts, loans or investments from family members when you're over 30. It just seems to be a bit more "sensitive" the older we all get.

This is especially true if you've gotten financial help before and failed to make good on your promises, whether to repay, put the money to good use, turn over a new leaf or whatever the case might be. But even if you did make good in the past it can still be uncomfortable for all parties when you "return to the same well."

ARE THEY WILLING AND ABLE?

I realize you might not have any family members you can ask for help. I'm sorry to say that many people don't. Whether you're simply alone in the world or are currently distant or estranged from your family, there are times this option is simply not realistic.

I also realize the idea of financial assistance from your family might seem like a cruel joke, because of your family's financial condition. Trust me, I know how many people are barely making ends meet these days because I've talked with them and tried to help them. There are millions of Americans in serious financial distress today who are unable to help their family members.

I talked with a little old lady named Miriam, for instance, who can't afford her medications and can barely buy food for herself because she spends almost every nickel she gets on her credit card bills. (And she refuses to skip payments or try anything different to ease her predicament.) So if she's your mother or grandmother I understand she's not flying in for your rescue.

So we know that millions of family members are not able to help their loved ones with debt. But millions of others are.

If you think yours are able, the question becomes, how able are they? If they have to dig into precious retirement savings or use their credit cards to help you, then they're probably not able enough. I've spoken with far too many parents who have become mired in debt by trying to help family members dig out of *their* debt. So be careful who you ask, for their sake and for yours.

The other question is whether your family members are willing even if they are able. Some practically wave a banner letting you know their answer is "Hell no!" It's their well-known family policy.

Other people have other policies. I know some will help in case of sickness or injury or even in case of an honest job loss, but would give a hard pass on helping with basic credit card debt. You have to know who you're dealing with.

EVERY SITUATION IS UNIQUE

I was 42 when I crashed, burned and almost skidded off the runway after losing the high-flying sports media position I told you about in Chapter One. So I was a little old to be asking my parents for help. And yet I could have.

My parents were healthy, happy and lived just a few miles away in our hometown area. They were actively involved with me and my family, they had plenty of money and they had been willing to help in the past.

And that's exactly why I couldn't ask.

They had been so generous in so many ways. They had given me my mother's old car after college and had even delivered it to me after I flew away to play pro football. They had shared some inheritance money with me and my brothers a number of years later. They had even offered to help me and my family during costly moves or transitions a couple times before.

So I was determined to leave them out of my painful mess, probably as much out of shame and embarrassment as nobility or heroism.

I've told you what debt had done to my mind and emotions at that time. Looking back, I regret several things including my isolation and do-it-myself outlook. Perhaps it was just my twisted pride at work. Whatever the case, I refused to reach out for help from family members, friends, mentors or financial coaches.

What I could have done then and what I advise clients to do now when circumstances recommend a conversation with their family members is to organize their thoughts in the following way.

A CAPTIVATING PROPOSAL

Rather than approach family members or friends with a woeful story, a defeated spirit and an outstretched hand begging for help, I recommend you "flip the script" and create *an informal presentation* that follows the outline of this book and reflects the ASAP Protocol.

Let's review what that means.

We can start with a quick look at this book's Table of Contents. Go back to that page if you can and take a look at how it's structured into three sections and then come back and we'll continue. Okay? Now go ahead and take a look!

Now that you're back, I hope you saw there are 15 chapters broken into three main sections labeled Your Condition, Your Options and Your Plan, right?

This follows our protocol for assessing your situation, reviewing your options and creating your best plan.

This is exactly how I recommend you organize a simple presentation about your finances with whoever you might ask for help. (I say "might" because I suggest you don't actually ask for help until you can gauge your audience's reaction to your presentation.)

You can tell them you're looking for their advice and feedback on an important financial matter and then present the following outline:

I. Your Condition:
- You briefly explain how you fell into debt.
- You present your four X-factor reports showing your debt load, net worth, P&L and FICO score.
- You share something about your financial mindset, spirit and vision for the future.

II. Your Options:
- You summarize the options you've reviewed and explain why you're seeking a low interest consolidation loan (for example).

III. Your Game Plan:
- You share your goal to secure a consolidation loan privately or to secure a trusted person to co-sign a loan with you at a bank.
- You explain your plan to secure coaching support to ensure your follow-through and success.
- You reinforce your financial vision for the future, including paying off the consolidation loan within 36 to 60 months depending on what's available, fastest and most manageable.

Chances are your family members will be blown away by your presentation and will offer to help in some meaningful way, shape or form. Why? Because your honesty, preparation and perspective will be impressive! And these qualities speak to the fears most family members have about helping loved ones, namely that they're disorganized and have no serious plans or vision for success. And if they don't volunteer to help you, you can ask them to help if you feel comfortable doing so.

It helps to remember that people often won't act unless they're asked. Salespeople know they normally have to ask for a sale and they know many customers actually want to be asked. Maybe you've even heard people say, "You have not because you ask not." So don't be afraid to ask.

What do you do if your family cannot or will not help you?

No problem. You simply shift your focus back to one of the options we outlined before this chapter or to one of them coming up after you turn the page. Either way, you're going to pick a proven approach and make it work.

SUMMARY:

The Option: Family Assistance

The Concept: Present your situation, your options and your plan to loved ones who are potentially willing and able to help.

Best Benefit: Immediate way to reduce monthly overhead and raise your FICO.

FICO Effect: It depends on the assistance you receive but personal gifts or private loans can dramatically help you reduce your debt load and raise your FICO score.

Best Suited: For debtors with family members willing and able to help.

Other Notes: If family members offer you a loan make sure to write up a simple agreement stating the terms and conditions for both of you to sign and retain copies. And if they offer you an interest-free loan I recommend you offer to pay at least nominal interest. It won't affect your monthly payment very much and it will express your appreciation in a tangible way that honors the value of their money.

CHAPTER NINE
Debt Settlement

"Can I ask you a few questions?" asked a 50-something gentleman named Jim.

"Of course," I replied, "go ahead."

"Okay, my first question is I why I'm getting flooded with mail from a million different lenders and debt-relief companies. How do they know my financial situation? Isn't my information private?"

"Well it depends on the privacy policies of your creditors," I said, "which of course is buried in fine print. But in most cases everyone's financial information is available to companies in some form."

"Okay, that figures," he said. "But why are they offering me loans that I know I can't qualify for? Why are they wasting their money on me?"

"They might be debt-settlement companies pretending to offer loans," I answered. "To raise your hopes and get you to respond."

"So they're scams," he growled.

"When they do that they are, yes!" I confirmed. "It's your basic "bait and switch" but it's hard to prove damages especially when they make a token effort to "find you a loan" before they present their real agenda."

"Okay, I get it." He said, as he thought through the crafty mechanics.

"But there are some reputable debt-settlement companies that play it straight," I added. "So I don't want to bad-mouth the entire industry or the whole debt-settlement approach, sometimes it's the right fit."

"Hmm." He replied. "Well I don't want to do bankruptcy, so can you explain how settlement works?"

"Sure," I said. "There are two ways to do it and both can work. But neither one is for the faint of heart."

DIY DEBT SETTLEMENT

In most cases debt settlement becomes an option when other debt-relief options won't work. Your debt load is too high or your income is too low to handle your own payoff plan, to qualify for a consolidation loan or payment plan or to afford even a hardship program. You're behind on your payments and there is no family rescue coming your way.

As in Jim's case, debt settlement is frequently considered a "last resort" alternative to bankruptcy.

The do-it-yourself (DIY) approach to debt settlement is straightforward. You contact your creditors directly and negotiate reduced settlement amounts, usually around 40% to 50% of your total past due balance.

While this approach may sound easy and attractive it can be time-consuming as you make calls, wait on hold, get transferred, dropped, questioned and finally speak with a negotiator and review, sign and return documents and pay a sizable lump sum settlement amount (or a series of scheduled payments if allowed).

When you multiply and repeat these efforts with each and every one of your creditors it can feel like a part-time job if you have a handful or more of them.

So when and why are creditors willing to settle?

Each creditor has their own timeline, but most will "charge-off" your debt within 90 to 180 days of your first missed payment. This means they write it off as a loss for tax purposes, while still working to collect some or all of your outstanding balance either directly or by selling your debt to another collector.

Just to be clear, creditors will not negotiate a settlement if you are current on your monthly payments or if you are just a couple of months behind. Most will only begin to consider a settlement after three or more missed payments, and some will actually send you a notice to offer or explore a settlement when they reach that point.

Most creditors will require a genuine hardship explanation from you about your default, so be prepared to share your Chapter Two background story.

THE FICO EFFECT

How do settlements affect your FICO score? Settlements are quite damaging to your credit because your score suffers from both your late payment and charge-off reports on your credit history for each account and from your eventual "Settled for less than the full amount" notation for each settled account. This notation will appear on your credit report for seven years and then drop off. Meanwhile a settlement's negative impact to your FICO score will decline after three years.

How bad is the immediate damage to your FICO score? Like so many other things regarding personal finances "it depends."

If Person A settles five maxed-out credit cards but stays current on her long-standing car, home and personal loans plus another ten credit cards with low balances, the negative impact could be just 50 to 100 points. I've seen cases like this where settlements – and even unsettled charge-offs – were not devastating because they were balanced by a good number of positive accounts with long and healthy histories.

Meanwhile if Person B's five settled credit cards are not offset by a car, home or personal loans or other healthy credit cards, the negative impact will be a lot more dramatic because there are no account histories to offset the damage.

These are moot points for most people, however, since the vast majority of people seeking debt settlements already have such bad debt-to-income ratios that even if they still have decent credit scores they are worthless for borrowing. Their debt load is simply too high to gain any kind of loan approval.

The alternate case is their FICO scores are already so damaged by late or missed payments that they're simply looking for a workable way to resolve impossible debts.

There is one bright spot I like to share with people considering debt settlement. I tell them future creditors who see settlements on their credit history will at least respect their goodwill efforts to work with their creditors to resolve their debts. It certainly looks better than unresolved charge-offs or bankruptcy and will often prompt creditors to ask "what happened?" They do so because industry insiders know that most settlements are negotiated by debtors in distress from unfortunate, unforeseeable or unavoidable losses or set-backs.

If nothing else, debt settlements can tidy up very messy credit reports while avoiding the stigma of bankruptcy.

DEBT SETTLEMENT COMPANIES

This is the "done for you" alternative to the DIY debt settlement approach.

Debt settlement companies handle settlement negotiations and payoffs for you in a process that usually takes 24 to 48 months. During this process you deposit funds each month – instead of making payments to creditors – into a secure third party escrow account in your name. The more you can afford to deposit each month the faster the settlement process can go.

These payments typically cut your normal monthly minimums in half, providing significant financial relief for you and your household.

As soon as sufficient funds build up in your escrow account, your settlement company will negotiate with one or more of your creditors, frequently the smallest balance or other accounts that are attractive for other reasons.

Such reasons can include insider knowledge about a particular creditor's readiness to negotiate or even about a creditor's legal threats to sue you (in which case you need an immediate response). There might also be a large-scale bundled or "bulk" settlement involving your account plus numerous other client accounts managed by your settlement company, with one of your creditors to provide you with exceptional savings.

How much do you save by settling your debts through a settlement company? Normally about 10% less than you would by negotiating them yourself. In other words you can save *more* by negotiating for yourself in most cases.

This is true because settlement companies can usually settle your debt for about 40% of what you owe, but you will pay around 60% after covering the settlement company's fee of roughly 20% of each transaction. They do not charge any other fees and they do not keep your escrow account funds if you ever decide to cancel your program. That money would return to you.

Bear in mind that not all creditors or debt settlement companies settle or charge fees to match the ballpark figures stated above and you should know some creditors have been known to refuse settlements altogether.

This is why "it depends" is such a common mantra in personal finance generally and debt settlement specifically and why you'll need to ask about fees and settlement expectations with your chosen company. This is also why you'll want to confirm that they can successfully negotiate with each of your targeted creditors before you sign up with them.

SUMMARY

The Option: Debt Settlement

The Concept: Negotiate reduced debt payoff amounts, either directly or by working through a settlement company.

Best Benefit: A dramatic reduction of your monthly overhead and debt balances.

FICO Effect: Significant damage from skipped payments and "charge-off" status until settlements are negotiated, with residual effects for seven years with some recovery possible within 24 to 36 months.

Best Suited: For debtors buried by impossible debt and/or behind on payments.

Other Notes: Remember to ask questions and confirm expectations if you sign with a debt settlement company, especially about negotiating with your targeted creditors. And be advised: Some creditors will not wait for your settlement company to negotiate with them and may file lawsuits against you to force collection, garnish your wages, etc. A good settlement company can help you respond properly and/or accelerate their efforts to negotiate with such creditors, but it's something to discuss up front as a worst-case scenario.

CHAPTER TEN
Bankruptcy Chapters 7 & 13

"Hey, honeybunch," I said to my wife and former high school sweetheart. "We really need to talk about our finances."

"Oh, no," she replied with slumped shoulders, already discouraged.

She had hoped and prayed I would get the high-paying CEO position in Knoxville that I wrote about back in Chapter One, especially after she had been invited to join me on my second visit to address their board of directors, as the final step in their executive search process.

So she was crushed when I didn't get the job.

She was also exhausted from her daily commute from our home in the South Bay area of L.A. all the way to Watts in South Central Los Angeles where she taught elementary school, with all the demands that came with her work.

But most of all she was tired of bill collector phone calls and financial stress.

"Look," I said, as calmly and confidently as I could. "You know we can't keep up with our consolidation program and I've tried to find something else, but..."

"What? " she interrupted me, her voice rising and cracking at the same time. "You want to do bankruptcy?"

Now I had the slumped shoulders.

"Well," I said, mustering what little conviction I possessed. "I think it's our best option, all things considered. Our best shot at a fresh start."

After some serious Q&A about how the process would work, she finally agreed and said, "Fine. Might as well bite the bullet and get it over with."

THE NUTS 'N BOLTS OF BANKRUPTCY

Let me start by saying that bankruptcy laws have changed since we went through the process, making it more difficult, more expensive and less forgiving. We can thank the banks for all that since they lobbied lawmakers to protect their interests and reduce their risks by passing new bankruptcy laws.

They didn't want debtors getting off "too easy."

Bankruptcy is still a viable option for certain situations, however. So how does it work?

There are two kinds of bankruptcy for individuals, known as Chapter 7 and Chapter 13. Each one means you are going to court to seek protection from your creditors to resolve your debts, normally with the help of a bankruptcy attorney. But each approach has requirements we'll discuss momentarily.

Here are some basics to know about the bankruptcy process:

1. You must complete a certified credit counseling course before you can file, and then you must complete another education course before your case is discharged.

2. You must pay court costs ($335 for Chapter 7, $310 for Chapter 13) and usually attorney's fees (figure $1,500 for Chapter 7, $3,000 for Chapter 13) to file. If you cannot afford these fees you can seek out free or discounted legal services in your community or contact successful

law firms and ask if they offer 'pro bono' (Latin for "for the public good") services to help with your bankruptcy filing.

3. You have to meet certain qualifications to file either Chapter 7 or 13.

4. Chapter 7 bankruptcy is a quick 6-month liquidation process for lower income debtors.

5. Chapter 13 bankruptcy is a 36 to 60 month restructured payment program for debtors with higher income and/or assets.

6. You stop all debt-collection activities and/or legal actions against you by filing.

7. You surrender control of your finances to a judge and/or trustee by filing.

8. You must continue paying child support, alimony, student loans and back taxes during and after your bankruptcy proceedings, they don't go away.

9. Your bankruptcy can appear on your credit report for up to 7 years after filing a Chapter 13 and up to 10 years after filing a Chapter 7 but it's generally no more devastating than having multiple accounts showing late payments or charge-offs.

10. You can normally rebuild your credit score within two years after bankruptcy.

CHAPTER 7 BANKRUPTCY – CLEAN, QUICK & SIMPLE

Chapter 7 bankruptcy is designed to be a clean and simple way to eliminate debt within six months but it's reserved for debtors with household incomes under their state's median income level. This is something determined through a "means test" you take before you file to make sure you qualify. It's basically a review of your debt load, net worth and P&L.

If the means test calculations indicate you have too much disposable income for the program, it is called a "presumption of abuse" and you are then referred to the Chapter 13 bankruptcy program – unless you can prove that you have special circumstances that effectively reduce your income or increase your expenses.

If you do qualify for Chapter 7 your financial matters will be reviewed by a trustee of the court. The trustee will order you to use your cash or sell your assets to pay off as much of your outstanding debt as possible. This is why Chapter 7 bankruptcy is often called a "liquidation" program.

You do not have to use all of your money or assets, however. This is true because there are numerous bankruptcy exemptions built into the law. Every state has their own rules but in general you can keep a "reasonable" portion of your cash (typically 75% from normal income sources and some additional from other sources) plus motor vehicles, clothing, appliances, furnishings, jewelry, retirement savings or pension, and even a portion of your home equity up to certain limits if you own a home. Luxury items are not exempt and can be sold by the trustee.

Once your non-exempt assets are used to pay off your debts, whether fully, partially or not at all, the court will discharge any remaining debt at that point. This could be any amount of debt, large or small.

If you still have outstanding (secured) debts like cars or properties in distress they can still be repossessed or foreclosed upon by your creditors once your bankruptcy proceedings are completed.

My experience with Chapter 7 bankruptcy was painful but positive. My lack of income at that time qualified us for the program and since we were renting a home and had no non-exempt assets we paid almost nothing to discharge over $50,000 of unsecured debt. And since I filed and managed our case 'pro se' (Latin for "on your own behalf") our legal costs were minimal.

I must confess it was stressful to complete and submit the documents myself, however, since it was foreign territory for me as a non-lawyer. As a result I was sweating the process every step of the way while trying to follow the official instructions, even though I had submitted legal forms for business activities in the past. So make sure you're comfortable with the official guidelines if you want to consider filing 'pro se.'

The most painful part for us came after the bankruptcy when I had to turn in the beautiful SUV I had given my wife as a birthday present just a couple years earlier, when the time for repossession drew near. That was our most tangible signal of surrender and defeat. But it was the price of our new beginning.

CHAPTER 13 BANKRUPTCY – A CHANCE TO REORGANIZE

Have you ever heard about a company that declared bankruptcy but rather than close their doors and liquidate everything they kept on doing business and seemed to be just fine? That's a Chapter 11 bankruptcy for corporations and it's a lot like a Chapter 13 bankruptcy for individuals.

Filing Chapter 13 bankruptcy stops all creditor actions behind the scenes, from collection calls to home foreclosures to repossessions of every kind, giving you time to create a modified payment plan for your creditors. This repayment or 'workout' plan is presented to the judge or trustee of the court for their approval or revision and ultimately for their supervision. (Remember, this doesn't halt payments for child support, alimony, student loans or taxes, as previously stated.)

The court will carefully assess your financial status (debt load, net worth and P&L), bank accounts and past tax returns to ensure that you dedicate a reasonable amount of your disposable income to satisfy your debts sufficiently within 36 to 60 months, to the best of your ability. As such you remain under the supervision of the court throughout this bankruptcy process.

The court prioritizes debt repayment in the following way and will make sure you pay top priority claims fully even if you pay only a portion (or none) of lower priority debts, as determined by the discretion of the court:

1. Priority Claims: Court costs and taxes
2. Secured Claims: Debts secured by collateral such as cars, homes and equipment
3. Unsecured Claims: Debts including credit cards and personal loans

The bottom line for Chapter 13 bankruptcy is that you keep your assets, gain protection and relieve financial pressure in exchange for damaging your credit score and surrendering some control of your finances to the court.

SUMMARY

The Option: Bankruptcy Chapters 7 and 13

The Concept: Seek legal protection to resolve overwhelming debt.

Best Benefit: An orderly process to resolve financial chaos.

FICO Effect: Significant damage from a bankruptcy filing, with residual effects for 7-10 years but some recovery possible within 24 to 60 months.

Best Suited: For debtors buried by impossible debt and/or behind on payments.

Other Notes: Seek legal or other knowledgeable counsel to assess your situation and qualifications for bankruptcy and to review the process. Remember to seek free, 'pro-bono' or discounted legal assistance if you cannot afford to hire an attorney and are not comfortable trying to handle your own case 'pro se.' And feel free to check with us for referrals or other assistance.

CHAPTER ELEVEN

Status Quo (Do Nothing)

"I think it's time for me to clean up my debt," proclaimed Walter, a friendly retired gentleman.

"Okay," I said, "how much debt are you dealing with?"

"I'm not exactly sure," he admitted, "but I know it's a lot!"

"Okay," I replied, knowing one person's idea of "a lot" is $5,000 while another person's might be $105,000. "Are you current on your payments?"

"Oh, heck no," he said, laughing, "It's been years since I've paid any of them!"

"Okay, then!" I joined his laughter for a moment.

"Do they still try to collect?" I wondered. "Has anyone tried to sue you?"

"No," he said to both questions.

"Hmm," I said as I reflected on similar situations I had run across before. "What kind of income do you have?"

"About thirteen hundred a month, Social Security," he said.

"Okay," I said, sadly reminded how many seniors live on so little retirement income. "And do you rent or own?" I asked as I neared a verdict on his case.

"Just rent this little apartment I've had for ten years," he replied.

"Well, Walter, here's the good news," I said. "Without digging into your credit history or stirring up old ghosts from the past it sounds like your accounts were charged off, written off and forgotten."

He listened silently.

"And because you don't have assets or attachable income," I explained, "they have no reason to take action. And neither do you, really."

'Okay," he said as he let everything sink in. "So I don't have to do anything?"

"No," I answered. "Now I will say your desire to address your old debt is commendable. But unless you have a pile of gold stashed somewhere to pay off old debts or you want to contact old creditors and pay them whatever you can afford, or unless you have some pressing need to rebuild your credit, then you'll be fine to leave things alone. You can relax and do nothing."

"Oh, okay," he said, happy for the insight. "Then that's what I'll do. Thanks!"

OTHER 'DO-NOTHING' SITUATIONS

Not all "do-nothing" situations involve long-forgotten debts or senior citizens with limited income or assets. Many involve much younger people struggling with debt but also with extenuating circumstances.

Sometimes sticking with the status quo (Latin for "the state in which") is just temporary, such as when you're behind on payments but not far enough behind yet to qualify for a consolidation program or settlement plan. In either case you may need to sit tight and do nothing as you miss payments and suffer further damage to your credit before you can qualify for a consolidation or settlement program.

Other times you might need to sit pat or "wait and see" for something else to happen. I've advised people waiting to receive financial settlements for instance and others waiting for a possible new job to come through or waiting to see if someone will help them or if something else will change, whether a spouse's promotion, raise, bonus or even a possible job loss. Life is full of variables that can dictate a temporary if not permanent "hold."

A close sister to the status quo approach is the "Don't mess things up" program. This can be the go-to approach when people want to buy a home but have debt to address first.

Imagine that Kendal and Kristen want to buy a house ASAP and they both have good jobs, but they have too much debt to qualify for a loan.

Now imagine they've heard magical things from friends or commercials about debt settlement and are considering that option. Is that a smart move?

No! The settlement process would typically take 24 to 48 months and it would damage their credit scores in the ways we outlined in Chapter Ten.

Kendal and Kristen's situation requires a careful strategy to reduce or eliminate debt as quickly as possible without doing anything to hurt their overall financial profile. This would be the time for an aggressive old-school payoff plan supplemented by reduced P&L expenses to free up cash-flow to pay down debt and improve their debt-to-income (DTI) ratio.

It would also be time to consider liquidating assets like boats or motorcycles to retire debt and/or add some overtime, part-time or side-hustle income to help pay down debt to qualify for their home loan.

This could also be a strategic time to request family assistance, using the ASAP Protocol format I recommended in Chapter Nine, only this time with the positive spin of helping to acquire a valuable real estate asset.

Every debt-relief situation is unique, so the status quo option is always something to keep in mind.

SUMMARY

The Option: Status Quo (Do Nothing)

The Concept: When doing nothing is the smartest move.

Best Benefit: Avoid unnecessary or harmful financial alternatives.

Best Suited: For debtors who have nothing to lose or need to "wait 'n see."

FICO Effect: Usually minimal but depends on circumstances.

Other Notes: Seek legal or knowledgeable counsel to assess your situation to ensure that making no move is your best move.

If you would like a free cheat sheet summary of this section's 7 debt solutions, you can request a copy at 7DebtSolutions.com.

PART III

YOUR PLAN

CHAPTER TWELVE

Pick an Option, Create a Plan

"So what do you recommend?" asked Katrina, a thirty-three-year-old medical equipment sales rep who ran up over $50,000 of credit card debt opening a home goods boutique/coffee shop "dream business" that she later had to shut down.

We had carefully reviewed her debt load, net worth, P&L and FICO and it was a mixed bag. She had a good income to go along with her hefty debt load, a slightly negative net worth, a strained but steady P&L and a 650 FICO score.

"My fiancé is nervous about getting married with all my debt," she added.

"I totally understand," I said as I considered all the variables she had shared. "Which of the debt-relief options we discussed struck the most positive chord with you?" I asked.

"I already got turned down for a consolidation loan," she said. "Definitely not bankruptcy or debt settlement," she added with certainty. "Both would ruin my credit and tangle me up for years because I would have to do Chapter 13, right?"

"Right," I confirmed. "Your income is too high for Chapter 7."

"Right," she echoed.

"So?" I prodded.

"I would say family assistance, but my parents are already digging into savings to help fund my wedding," she said. "And the old-school payment plan is going to take forever. I feel totally stuck."

"Not necessarily forever." I said.

"What do you mean?" she asked.

"I see a couple of possible scenarios depending on how you want to play it." She remained quiet so I continued.

"For instance, you could scale back on your wedding costs and talk to your parents about maybe gifting the money to pay off your debt instead. Or they might be willing to co-sign a low interest loan with you to consolidate your debt."

"Hmm." she said, thinking. "Probably too late to scale back the wedding, but they might consider co-signing a loan with me."

"Okay, so that's one possibility," I said. "The other option would require some old-fashioned belt-tightening on your part."

"How much tightening?"

"Well, you have good income, but I noticed most of it is going toward your relatively expensive apartment, your car and travel," I said, recalling her Range Rover lease of almost a thousand dollars a month.

"I see way too many people maxed out because of expensive car payments," I added. "You can explore trading out of it to save a few hundred bucks a month that you could use to pay down debt. Same goes for dialing back your travel. And you'll be saving a bunch on rent when you guys move in together so that will help you pay down your debt a lot faster if you stay focused."

"Yeah, my lease is almost up so I can turn it in and get a used Audi or something pretty nice for like half as much," she affirmed. "And sharing rent and cutting back on travel could definitely help," she said optimistically.

"Yup, definitely," I affirmed.

"Okay, so what's my plan, then?" She sounded ready and determined.

"Well here's how I would lay it out for your fiancé," I said. "Start with the big picture. Tell him you're going to follow a proven 'old-school' payoff plan. You're going to chop your debt down to size ASAP, first by cutting your car payment in half and using the difference each month to pay off debt. You're also going to cut your travel in half, or by whatever amount you can commit to, right?"

"Right," she said, tracking with me and taking notes.

"You're also going to save money on rent that you will use to pay down debt." I reminded her. "And you've got two aces up your sleeve."

"Really?" she wondered.

"Yes, the first one is that your FICO score will skyrocket as you aggressively pay down debt, qualifying you for a low interest consolidation loan within 6 to 9 months, which you can use to get rid of your remaining high interest balances. That will lower your overhead further and speed up your debt-elimination plan even more."

"Wow, I like it!" she said. "This gives me hope. And I think he'll like it."

"Your second ace is your parents. You can share your situation and your plan with them if you like, whether now or later, and see if they'd like to help. Or you can hold off on that and view that as a fallback or emergency plan."

"Yeah, I'd rather not stress them out any more than they already are with the wedding," she said.

"Okay, so there you go," I said. "I think you got this."

"Yeah, me too," she said. "I think I got this."

TIME TO DEBRIEF

This is a typical consultation and by "typical" I mean unique. Every person and situation is different, even when they're similar to others in some way. In this case Katrina was fortunate to have a solid income, affluent family members and options that quickly separated themselves from the pack.

I wanted to share this longer conversation to give you a feel for the decision-making process. And it is a process.

Our ASAP Protocol is the simple 3-step process we follow to assess basic background factors, review debt-relief options and determine your best plan.

The approach may seem cut and dried, but of course it's not because there are emotional and other variables involved with every situation. And that's why I love the process so much and encourage you to embrace it as well.

Creative solutions can usually be found when you're willing to dig around for them.

Did you notice Katrina's initial mental block? She felt stuck, hopeless and under serious time pressure to find a solution. That's what $50,000 of debt staring you in the face every month will do to you, especially when monumental events or life-changing transitions are bearing down on you.

Most people don't perform well under pressure and debt applies its fair share of it. So we don't see obvious solutions hiding in plain sight, such as where or how to cut costs, liquidate assets, organize things differently or reach out for help.

And it's not easy or natural to think creatively about our own lives because we become "hard baked" into our routines, habits and thought patterns. This is why we need help from trusted advisors, mentors, family members or coaches.

We all need fresh perspective from knowledgeable guides.

THE POWER OF A PLAN

Everything starts with vision. You might remember our discussion about vision back in Chapter Four and how vision naturally produces goals that in turn produce plans to accomplish them.

One of the examples I shared was President John F. Kennedy's vision to land American astronauts on the moon. That vision produced the concrete goal of doing it by the end of the decade back in the 1960s. In turn that "impossible" goal produced amazing plans to make it happen and get it done.

Katrina's vision wasn't exactly clear but at least she was looking to deal with her debt. Her goal was to do that, or at least figure out *how* to do that, before her wedding, to address her fiancé's concerns. And her plan emerged from those dynamics as she reached out for guidance that offered viable options and a concrete path for her to follow and it gave her a boost of remarkable confidence.

Did you notice how dramatically a plan changed her outlook? Her circumstances didn't change but her mindset and resulting plan changed her outlook – and ultimately her life – in a dramatic way.

Now let's review your situation and options once again to help you pick your best option to create a winning plan.

How did you fall into your current struggle with debt? What is your debt load? What is your net worth? Do you have assets you can sell or leverage to eliminate debt? How does your P&L look? Do you see places to cut costs or increase revenue to help pay down your debt? What is your FICO score and how does it limit or empower you as you consider your best options?

1. **The Hi-Low Payoff Plan** can be your best solution if your income is steady, you are current with your payments and you want to improve your FICO score and get rid of your debt. Re-read Chapter Five to refresh your memory on this approach and review Chapter Three's sections on Debt Load and P&L.

Your real plan here is to get organized and establish a system you can follow. Look carefully at your account balances, monthly payments and interest rates. Do you have a low balance you can pay off quickly to get the ball rolling? Or is there a hefty installment loan payment you can eliminate that will release more cash flow for you to pay down other debts?

Your plan here is:

a. Organize and study your Debt Load and P&L.

b. Look for ways to increase your income and reduce your expenses.

c. Target your priority accounts.

d. Take aim and pay them off ASAP!

e. Celebrate your victory, stay focused and repeat the process.

2. **Debt Consolidation** is a no-brainer if you can qualify for a low interest loan or balance transfer card to pay off higher-interest debt. If so your next step is to apply and carry on from there. If you cannot qualify or are already running behind on your monthly payments (and thus, already damaging your credit) you can select a consolidation/debt management program to lower your monthly overhead and simplify your financial affairs.

Review Chapter Six again to clarify your plan. You're going to get a consolidation loan, transfer your balances to a 0% card or sign up with a debt-consolidation/management company. Feel free to contact us for referrals.

3. **A Hardship Payment Plan** makes sense if you've fallen behind on your payments, can't catch up, and don't mind coordinating with each of your creditors to close your accounts and/or arrange a forbearance or payment deferral program or to reduce your interest or payments with them. Chapter Seven is where you can review this approach.

   Your plan here is:
   a. Organize and study your Debt Load in detail.
   b. Create a file for notes, statements, etc.
   c. Contact your creditors as recommended in Chapter Seven.
   d. Take notes and collect documents.
   e. Celebrate each agreement, stay focused and stick with your plan until the debts are paid off.

4. **Family Assistance** can rescue you from distress and spare you from damaging your credit. But be careful to approach family the right way if you think they might be willing and able to help. Check out Chapter Eight to review my recommended steps for this plan.

5. **Debt Settlement** may be your best bet if you have some income but not nearly enough to keep up with your payments. This is often the last resort to avoid bankruptcy while dramatically discounting your monthly payments and debt balances through negotiated settlements. Be sure to review Chapter Nine. You can contact a settlement company of your choice or request a referral from us. If you'll be negotiating settlements directly with creditors your plan is below.

a. Organize and study your Debt Load list of accounts.

b. Create a file for notes, statements, etc.

c. Contact your creditors' settlement departments.

d. Share your story and negotiate your best settlements.

e. Celebrate each settlement, stay focused and stick with your plan until the debts are paid off.

6. **Bankruptcy** is the last resort for most people, but it may be the perfect solution for you and your situation. You'll need some money to file and pay an attorney (unless you can file your case 'pro se' or locate free or *pro bono* legal services) but it's a sure way to freeze creditor actions and get rid of your debt. Take another tour of Chapter Ten to polish your plan. And feel free to contact us for a referral.

7. The **Status Quo** approach is the way to go when your circumstances suggest you do nothing. Be sure to revisit Chapter Eleven for more on this.

CHAPTER THIRTEEN

Scams, Cars, Collection Calls & More

"So where do we address some of the most common questions and topics that come up during conversations about debt?" I asked myself.

This is where I decided we should tackle some miscellaneous topics that didn't quite fit in previous chapters but may fit into your game plan going forward. We'll address them through the following Q&A format.

Q: How do you avoid debt-relief or credit-related scams?

A: 1. Throw away junk mail offering loans or debt relief.

2. Don't answer calls from unknown callers or numbers.

3. If you accidentally answer, just politely decline any conversation about financial matters and hang up, especially if the callers sound foreign or if you can hear the background noise of a "boiler room" call center. Scam operators commonly use cheap foreign call centers to "bird-dog" people in financial distress and earn commissions by transferring them to high-pressure debt-relief or settlement companies.

4. Don't believe anything sounding "too good to be true." It probably is.

5. Contact only reputable or recommended experts or advisors for financial assistance.

Q: How do I avoid car repossession if I'm behind on payments?

A: Your only real hope is to contact your lender to request a hardship payment plan or to negotiate one or more deferred or discounted payments.

If your lender has turned your past due account over to a collection agency you can talk with them but will probably have better luck speaking with your original lender or finance company to avoid losing your vehicle.

Q: Is it possible to stop debt-collection calls?

A: Yes. You can send a letter to creditors by mail asking them to cease and desist all further phone communication. Be sure to keep a copy of this letter. You should send it by certified mail and pay for a "return receipt" for your records as well. Once a collector gets your letter, they can only contact you to confirm they will stop contacting you or to inform you of a specific action like filing a lawsuit against you. If you are represented by an attorney and you inform the collector of that fact, the collector must communicate only with your attorney (not you) unless your attorney fails to respond within a reasonable period of time to communication efforts from the collector.

For further information on debt-collection guidelines, restrictions and harassment claims go to the Federal Trade Commission's Consumer Information site at www.consumer.ftc.gov/articles/debt-collection-faqs.

Q: What should I do if I'm falling behind on my mortgage payments?

A: You should contact your mortgage loan servicer to discuss your situation and your options. At the time of this writing the government's CARES Act offers 6 to12 months of homeowner relief through loan forbearance, which allows you to skip payments during that period. Time will tell if/how this program is extended. If no special homeowner relief programs exist, you can explore a "loss mitigation" plan with your mortgage servicer to avoid the high cost of foreclosure to both you and them. They may offer forbearance, a repayment plan, short sale or loan modification (reducing your interest rate or extending the term of your loan to reduce your monthly payment) to help you keep your home while dealing with financial hardship.

You can also sell your home if you have equity in it or file for bankruptcy to protect your home while restructuring or eliminating other debts. As always, you are advised to get legal advice on such matters.

Q: How should I deal with overwhelming medical debt?

A: Many Americans are overwhelmed by medical bills they cannot pay and because the bills frequently accompany other financial hardships, they are simply ignored. This can lead to past due notices, negative reporting and impact on your FICO score and even legal action. Thankfully, many creditors in the medical field are flexible and reasonable to offers of partial payment. For this reason, I encourage clients to contact creditors directly if they are falling behind on their payments. In my experience, creditors will agree to almost any reasonable good faith offer to make payments and make progress.

Q: How should I deal with IRS taxes that I owe?

A: This is another situation people often ignore to their detriment because the IRS automatically charges interest and penalties on overdue/unpaid taxes and they can levy tax liens on properties and/or garnish the wages of taxpayers who don't respond to their "Intent to Levy" or other notices regarding unpaid taxes. In most cases your best solution is to contact the IRS directly to negotiate a payment plan to catch up on unpaid taxes over the course of 24 to 60 months. In serious hardship cases you can try to negotiate a reduced settlement with the IRS – usually handled by attorneys who specialize in this field called an Offer in Compromise (OIC). This approach is sometimes called The Fresh Start Initiative and has been streamlined to help distressed taxpayers qualify more quickly and easily. Even so, this program is not a fast or easy "slam dunk" for debtors. Some reports indicate only 20% of requests are ever settled. And beware of scams as unscrupulous lawyers and other tax advisors have been known to charge sizable up-front fees and then fail to complete the settlement process for their clients.

Q: Are payday loans or title loans a good idea in a pinch?

A: These loans are a terrible idea and an absolute last resort. They can charge 25% interest or more per month (that's $25 per month for every $100 borrowed) which equals 300% Annual Percentage Rate (APR). I have spoken with dozens of people who have fallen prey to these lenders who reportedly will not hesitate to come knocking on debtors' doors at night to collect on late or skipped payments, or to repossess vehicles used as collateral for title loans. Many such debtors get caught in a vicious cycle of owing most of whatever they earn each paycheck to pay off previous loans they used for emergencies or to bridge gaps they cannot escape.

Q: How do I deal with delinquent child support or alimony payments?

A: Whether you're the struggling payer or recipient in such cases, you will need to get legal enforcement or relief through the court if you cannot resolve the matter privately.

Q: What do I do if I'm sued for defaulting on a credit card?

A: First and foremost don't ignore the court summons as that can lead to a judgement in favor of the creditor and the garnishment of your wages or lien against your assets. It should prompt you to take one of these actions:

1. Contact the creditor's settlement department immediately to see if you can still negotiate a settlement before your court date.
2. Contact an attorney to file bankruptcy to protect you from the suit.
3. Prepare to attend your court hearing and present a settlement proposal to the judge based on a summary review of your circumstances.
4. Attend the court hearing, answer the judge's questions and take your chances with the court's ruling.

Q: What should I do if I'm 'underwater' on my car or home?

A: This really depends on your overall situation. In many cases having negative equity (i.e. owing more than your car or home is worth) is only temporary due to market conditions and may improve over time. And negative equity may not even impact your day-to-day finances or lifestyle if you can keep making payments and keep driving your car and/or living in your home. If you want to sell your car or home you will need to either 'roll' the negative equity into your new car (if the numbers make that possible) or sell your home 'short' or at a loss. There are other scenarios you can explore further with your lenders or with car sales, real estate or financial experts or with us at support@debt-freeasap.com.

Q: How can I get student loan relief?

A: Here are the leading student loan relief programs or approaches:

1. Loan Deferment – You can request loan deferment from your loan provider with no interest accrued during the deferment period if you are unemployed, dealing with financial hardship or are enrolled in school at least half-time.

2. Loan Forbearance – You can request to skip payments for up to 12 months at a time based on a variety of life or work situations, however interest will continue to accrue and some loan providers limit the total number of months forbearance is allowed.

3. Total and Permanent Disability Discharge (TPD) – This US Department of Education program forgives student loan debts for those who meet permanent disability requirements.

4. Income-Driven Repayment Plans – This kind of program allows you to request lower payments based on your

limited income and usually caps your repayment period at 20 or 25 years of payments and your monthly payment to 10% of your monthly income.

5. Public Service Loan Forgiveness (PSLF) Program – This program forgives up to $24,150 of student loan debt remaining after applicants make ten years' worth of payments on their student loans while working in qualified government or non-profit jobs or careers. This program will likely be modified soon since most applicants fail to meet qualifications and both parties in congress are floating revised debt forgiveness programs to address the student loan crisis. Stay tuned and check with us for updates.

CHAPTER FOURTEEN

The Support You Need to Succeed

"I am so discouraged," muttered Susan, a mid-forties mom trying to dig her family out of $38,000 worth of credit card debt.

She was sad and she was mad, mostly at herself.

"It's like that game where you hit the chipmunks that keep popping up from different holes," she said. "I keep swinging, but I keep missing."

"I hear you," I said. "That's called Whack-A-Mole, by the way."

"That's right!" she said. "I make progress in one area, and then something else pops up, an emergency, a moment of weakness, whatever."

"Hey, I totally understand," I said.

"My husband blames me for all the spending and thinks we should just file bankruptcy," she added. "What do you think?"

"I'm not sure," I replied. "Are you following a clear plan or systematic approach right now?"

"Kinda sorta," she answered.

"Do you have anyone helping you, someone in your corner to help keep you on track?" I asked. "Like maybe a family member or friend or someone at church or maybe even your accountant if you have one. Can you think of anyone?"

The phone went quiet for a moment, as I heard the sniffling that comes with someone fighting back tears.

"My nine-year-old son always tries to help me," she said, right before sobbing uncontrollably.

THE POWER OF SUPPORT

One of my favorite scriptures states that if a single warrior can send a thousand enemies to flight, two can send ten thousand.

I mention this "multiplier effect" because taking control of your finances and charting a new course toward financial freedom is fairly simple but it can be extremely challenging. And we all need help.

Remember where we started in Chapter One by counting the ways debt sucks life out of us financially, emotionally, mentally, relationally and spiritually? In most cases this means we are in a weakened and compromised state when we try to climb out of our debt.

How much easier it is when someone shines a light, throws you a rope or climbs along with you!

Even someone's encouraging voice can mean the difference between reaching the top and falling back into the void. And most of us understand this. This is why Weight Watchers and so many other successful weight-loss programs build coaching and community support into their programs.

And this is why I exhort you to seek out someone knowledgeable about debt relief and/or personal finances to mentor, support or coach you. I'm talking about someone who will consistently be there for you to encourage you and hold you accountable. I believe that having this advocate or supporter will increase your odds of success from well under 50-50 to something much closer to 100%.

This is also why I've built ongoing coaching support into our Debt-Free ASAP consultations and is the basis of our Debt-Free Forever program.

THE 7 VIRTUES OF COACHING

Why is coaching such a game-changer?

I could write a book on this subject and maybe this book is an indirect shot at doing that. But coaching matters, and here's why.

1. Society has changed. Extended families are fragmented. Village "elders" are not handy to dispense wisdom and direction. Privacy is highly valued so isolation is more common. Knowledgeable support is often less organic and more virtual, professional or transactional. Coaching is an old-school way to connect in a meaningful way.

2. Expertise is worth its weight in gold, and so is experience. So it often makes more sense to hire an expert than to research or learn a whole new subject yourself, especially when time is of the essence. And no matter what you might learn on your own, you will still lack practical experience. Coaching delivers both knowledge and experience to your area of need.

3. Discipline is required to engineer and reinforce change. Discipline is built on basics and repetition and focus. Discipline breeds an organized approach to anything, whether sports, art, music, science, building or personal finances. Coaching requires and promotes discipline.

4. Encouragement is desperately needed but often lacking and hard to find. My wife and I often marvel at how few people try to encourage, compliment or affirm others these days. Has encouragement become a lost art in this age of self- promotion, cyber-hate and trolling? Does it stem from our basic selfishness and insecurity or from the exhaustion of our everyday lives? Coaching can fill this encouragement gap.

5. Enthusiasm is contagious. The word itself conveys a lively or intense interest or all-consuming passion and it comes from the Greek word *enthousiasmos* which means 'filled by God's spirit.' My college football coach used to say, "Nothing great was ever accomplished without enthusiasm," and he was certainly right about that. Then again he also used to say, "It's a beautiful day on the playground!" every day before practice whether it was perfect fall sunshine, terribly hot and humid or rainy and cold. It's funny how I say the same things myself now so many years later. Coaching is "more caught than taught."

6. Fellowship is deeply felt. Coaches don't just teach or tell you what to do. They join you in your struggle and become vested supporters of your cause. They work with you, not above you and they celebrate your victories and mourn your defeats right alongside you. Coaching is fellowship in action.

7. Seasons come and go but results can last forever. You might see your same doctor or therapist for years, but you'll usually work with a coach for just a season. Coaches work for a specific time period or to achieve a specific result. Coaches want to see you turn it around, break through, win a championship, earn your license, lose 50 pounds, run your marathon, eliminate your debt or accomplish whatever you dream of doing or getting done. Coaching is all about timely (and lasting) results!

CHAPTER FIFTEEN

Keep Your Eyes on the Prize!

"I think we've got to throw in the towel," said Ken, a client of mine who had opted for a debt-settlement plan after suffering a heart attack that reduced his income and piled up medical and credit card debts. He had called to share more bad news.

"So Katie lost her job? I asked. "Is that temporary or permanent?"

"They don't know," he said. "The Pandemic pretty much wiped her company out."

"Wow," I said. "I'm really sorry to hear that."

"Yeah, she's getting some unemployment but there's no way we can keep up with our settlement payments."

"Have you talked with your creditors? I know some are offering to suspend payments during all this chaos," I said.

"Yeah, I don't know. Either way I think we're cooked with both of us taking such big hits," he said with resignation.

"What are you going to do?" I wondered.

"We'll just try to save the house for the time being, I guess," he surmised. "We're in total survival mode."

"Yeah, I hear you," I said, hating to let defeat win the day.

"Anyway, I thought you should know," he added, preparing to say goodbye.

"Well hold the phone, Ken," I said. "I know this is a terrible and massive set-back. But please don't let go of the rope. If you don't follow through with your debt now it will just get messier later. And you don't want to lose your house or deal with legal action coming your way, right?"

"Right. But what do you suggest?" he asked. "Bankruptcy? That's our worst nightmare."

"Maybe," I said. "I would first double-check your settlements and try to renegotiate or defer them. And if that won't work at least a bankruptcy would protect your home, relieve your pressure and help you adjust to whatever your 'new normal' is going to look like. And it would still eliminate your other debts as quickly and responsibly as anything else."

"That's true," he agreed. "Let me discuss it with Katie and call you back, okay?"

"Okay," I said. "Remember your goal. Your circumstances have changed but your ultimate goal doesn't have to."

HITTING THE WALL

Setbacks happen to everyone, especially when we're trying to take command of our lives, to climb higher, make moves, recover or dramatically change ourselves or our circumstances for the better. Stop smoking. Stop drinking. Stop gambling. Leave a bad job or relationship. Start a new career or business. Lose weight. Save money. Get more education. Give generously. Get a fresh start. Conquer debt.

It's easy to give up, especially when we're already beaten down.

I'm reminded of how many times I wanted to quit playing football during pre-season two-a-day practices over the years. Whether it was the wilting heat or dehydrating Santa Ana winds and the resulting "cotton mouth" in high school, the painful shin splints and punishing drills I endured in college or the high altitude gasping or God-forsaken humidity in my pro camps, something caused me to seriously consider quitting every year, to the point where I honestly told loved ones I had hit the wall and was done.

So why didn't I quit?

This takes us back to visions, goals and action plans. And in this case my vision or dream was just magnetic enough, my goals just compelling enough and the support of my loved ones just encouraging enough to keep me moving forward for one more day. And that was usually enough. My body would feel better, the weather would improve or I would have an especially good practice the next day.

Marathon runners have long talked about "hitting the wall."

This is the unavoidable 'bonk' experience runners must endure around miles 18-20 of every 26.2 mile marathon, when their glycogen energy levels are depleted, their legs feel like concrete due to fatigue and their minds are filled with doom, gloom and questions about why they ever wanted to run a marathon in the first place.

ON TO THE FINISH LINE

So how do marathon runners (or debt conquerors) break through the wall?

There are three major keys to success:

1. Preparation – For runners this means careful diet, exercise and mental training, usually over an extended period of time. They can't just roll out of bed one day and run a marathon the next! Same goes for debt conquerors. We have to take the proper steps and adopt the proper mindset knowing that becoming debt-free is a process, rarely

an overnight sensation or a quick sprint. (Even ASAP means *as soon as possible*, not instantly!) Most of us didn't fall into debt overnight, so it may take some time to climb out of it.

2. Planning – Successful marathon runners have a plan and they stick to it. They plan for the wall and regulate their pace accordingly by avoiding sudden energy-depleting spurts, for instance. They also plan to re-hydrate throughout the race and consume carbs as they run to keep their energy up. Successful debt conquerors can plan ahead as well, knowing the process will become tiresome. For this reason I suggest a steady stream of rewards or treats built into your plan to help you "stick with it" to the finish line, something we'll discuss further in a minute.

3. Support – Most successful marathoners have a support team of coaches, trainers, friends or family members to cheer them on, often at strategic points along the race course and especially around the wall. They know the value of enthusiastic support, encouragement and celebration as they rack up mile after mile on their course. Debt conquerors should know and do the same.

CELEBRATE VICTORY NOW AND THEN

Let me explain what I mean by this headline.

I'm not suggesting you celebrate "every now and then" as if to say you should celebrate only occasionally, casually or randomly.

What I mean to say is something more powerful and profound, I think, something I want to leave with you as a final encouragement.

These words will hopefully serve as a kind of "sonic boom" or exclamation mark reminder of what I've mentioned along the way concerning the debt recovery process and how it relates to your holistic health and well-being and to your vision, goals and mindset. So here it is.

When I say to "celebrate victory now and then" I mean to celebrate both the first mile and the twenty-sixth mile of the marathon at the same time, or to celebrate your first settlement (or consolidation payment or old-school payoff payment or whatever) and your last one *at the same time.* I'm talking kaboom!

What am I trying to say?

I want to encourage you to start celebrating your full-blown debt-free status right here and now, at mile one. Just look how far you've gotten in this book, and how far you've come in terms of insight and perspective since you started. Isn't it amazing how much you know right now?

You are loaded with explosive chain-breaking, life-changing knowledge and power.

To celebrate how far you have come – and to celebrate the person you've already *become* – I suggest you stand up and take a bow, raise your hands, do your happy dance, jump and shout, yell "boom!" or say "Halleluiah" for making it this far. Go ahead and do that!

And as you do I encourage you to 'see' and celebrate your ultimate destination and victory of becoming debt-free (and eventually wealthy) at the same time. See what I mean? Celebrate now *and* then, right here and now!

Remember how I talked about saying 'boom!' whenever I paid off a debt? That's the victorious destination, the end of every debt-conquering effort. But I also celebrated every time I made a plan or call, completed a form, a filing, a negotiation or payment to get there, maybe not out loud but at least inwardly to applaud my progress and determination. Step by step, one celebration, one fist-pump or high-five, one reward, one release of endorphins at a time as every celebration re-wired my mental and emotional circuitry for success.

You can get creative with your rewards, whether it's a Hershey's Kiss or a trip to the ice cream shop, the nail salon or some other kind of special treat or present to reinforce your new and better financial behavior. These little celebrations can change your life!

Hire a coach or recruit a mentor, mate or supporter to celebrate the steps of your journey with you and you'll be standing on the victory stand all proud and sexy with a gold medal around your neck and a list of zero balance accounts in your hand, basking in the glory that comes with true accomplishment, pride, victory and freedom in the blink of an eye. See it and celebrate it now as if it's then, and soon enough it will be.

You can do this. You can start now and become Debt-Free ASAP!

If you would like to learn about scheduling a personal consultation with me, and enjoy a $50 discount just for reading this book, please visit: Debt-FreeASAP.com/book-consult.

www.ingramcontent.com/pod-product-compliance
Lightning Source LLC
Chambersburg PA
CBHW072203100526
44589CB00015B/2342